BSA Bantam

Other titles in the Crowood MotoClassic Series

BSA BANTAM

Owen Wright

The Crowood Press

First published in 2003 by
The Crowood Press Ltd
Ramsbury, Marlborough
Wiltshire SN8 2HR

www.crowood.com

British Library Cataloguing-in-Publication Data
A catalogue record for this book is available from the British Library.

ISBN 1 86126 539 5

Designed and typeset by Focus Publishing, 11A St Botolph's Road, Sevenoaks, Kent TN13 3AJ

Printed and bound in Great Britain by Bookcraft, Midsomer Norton

Contents

Above *Owen Wright on a 1957 150cc D3 Bantam Major. (Owen Wright)*

Left *The famous BSA Bantam motif was applied to thousands of D1 models and familiar all over the world. (Owen Wright)*

Preface

I blew my first-ever wage packet on a BSA Bantam, a 1956 150cc model D3 Major. I was seven quid lighter, with a provisional licence and tie-on L-plates, and 866 RRE was mine. Little did I know that it was already a clapped-out hack, having been used by the Leicester-based Fosse Riders MCC to train hundreds of learners before being pinched and left for dead in the Grand Union Canal. It had been dragged from the water, tarted up and offered to me as an alternative to riding a clanky old bicycle.

Despite this inauspicious beginning, I was badly bitten by the motorbike bug and I have never recovered. Since those carefree days of riding to work in a boiler suit, toe-tector boots and an old leather jacket, I have always kept a collection of various motorcycles, mostly BSA of one sort or another. I have owned seven Bantams, five D3 Majors, an ex-GPO D1 and a late B175, all of them either bought in a rough second-hand condition and in need of attention, and sometimes nothing more than a box of bits and a rusty battered frame. I re-built them, rode them and eventually sold them in order to acquire something larger.

I had decided to leave Bantams alone, until an old friend phoned to say that he had recovered his father's old D1, and asked me if I could help. Then a D3 turned up, just the thing for my son to take on as a project. Before I knew it we were doing the autojumble circuit and spending weekends rummaging through old cardboard boxes and piles of rusty parts. People were walking away with Bantam frames, wheel rims and engines tucked under their arms, and gradually we began to see more and more fully restored Bantams entered into shows. It seems that the Bantam is back and perhaps now is a good time to tell the full story.

Information on Bantams tends to be spread over a wide range of sources. The history and technicalities of BSA's one and only success with the two-stroke engine is usually covered in just one chapter in a more broad-based title. This book aims to gather together everything to do with Bantams and explore the impact made by the Bantam both on the story of motorcycling and on Britain's social history. It is not meant to be a purely factual and intensely technical presentation, but an account of personal experiences that capture the spirit of the Bantam. Mention the Bantam in any kind of social or business situation, and usually someone will chip in with 'A Bantam? I had one of those!' Generally, they launch into a series of anecdotes about a small, delightful machine of which they have fond memories. Old Bantamites quickly become friends; it is a subject that easily breaks down barriers.

The Bantam story is not a glamorous one – it involves few celebrities and no film stars – but plenty of ordinary people rode them and experienced excitement and exhilaration, and occasional frustration and anguish. Perhaps the humble appeal of the BSA Bantam is explained by the rapid takeover of our lives by new technology. Riding a Bantam is the perfect antidote: it is a carefree and uncomplicated experience, and there is no silly little light to tell you the gears are in neutral. The Bantam is a simple mechanical contrivance that runs on the minimum of parts. Of all the motorcycles I ever owned, big and small, none ever gave me as much contentment and ease of mind as that first battered and bruised Bantam Major.

There are many 'what might have beens' in the Bantam story. Throughout its history there were numerous efforts to develop the basic Bantam, from Charley Salt's clutchless gear change to an entirely new engine with positive lubrication, but such developments always withered on the vine. Apart from the change from magneto to alternator electrics during the mid-1960s, the last Bantam was not that different from the first.

This book stays with the mainstream Bantams, the ones that we all bought and rode. It is not a service manual – it does not tell you how to strip the engine or how much air to pump into the back tyre – but it does aim to provide the inspiration for a restoration project.

Perhaps, like me, you have thrilled at the joy of the open road in top gear and getting lost in the countryside with no worldly worries, or suffered the lows of a bike that will not start, lights that do not work and the absence of anything resembling power reaching the back wheel. If you have, you probably share an old Bantamite's obsession for patronizing lost causes and a fatalistic sense of humour.

Keep shaking the tank, and enjoy your Bantam.

Owen Wright
March 2002

Acknowledgements

The BSA Bantam was a people's bike and this book was compiled from a thick file of letters, e-mails and scribbled notes from countless people who once rode, raced, fixed, fettled or fell off a Bantam. It is quite amazing that such a humble subject could bring back so many fond memories. To all the people who are not mentioned below but who made some unwitting contribution with a wry comment or anecdote, I remain eternally grateful.

Many people, variously connected with Bantams, deserve full praise. Without the kind and enthusiastic assistance of Alistair Cave, former BSA Small Heath works manager, this book would never have been attempted. Other ex-BSA personnel who helped to set some matters straight include Jack Dyson, John Garner, Peter Glover, Michael Martin, Chris Vincent and Ed Wright.

The idea for this book was kick-started long ago by the late John Clarke, who once sold me a very forlorn piece of rusty metal on wheels. Thirty years later, the throttle was fully opened by David Scott of Premier Signs, Rugby, who never knew quite what he had started when he phoned about his father's old Bantam. Getting the clutch and gears sorted in the right order is due to countless former Bantamites, young and old, although at times I dearly wished someone would slam on the brakes!

Special thanks go to Steve Foden of the BSA Owners Club, Eric Hathaway of the British Two-Stroke Club, and Annette Collett of the VMCC Library. Thanks also to Sheila Whittingham and all the ladies at WIMA – keep those wheels rolling! Much of the GPO Bantam information came courtesy of Chris Hogan and the Post Office Vehicle Club. Help on red ex-Postie Bantam matters was also graciously provided by John and Kate Lawrence.

From the Antipodes, where men once rode green and gold Bantams, help came from Stan Johns, Ned Kern and Tony (Mist Green never looked so good) Morisset.

The go-faster information was ably supplied by Neil Andrew, Roy Bacon, Mick Barr, Rex Caunt, Clive Dawkes and Paul Styles.

Good stories worth a book in themselves came from the pens of Ken Ascott, David Atkins, David Brindley, Denis Bryant, David Garside, Tony Haywood and John Storey. How I wish I could have included all their words.

Worthy advice and contributions were made by Brian 'Badger' Crichton of Classic Bike magazine; Max Nightingale of Alpha Bearings; Peter Hollins of The Leicester Mercury; John Dunn of Imperial Tobacco plc; and the Fosse Riders MCC, with special mention to Mike and Chris Fairhead.

I must also thank my wife Susan (again), whose patience and understanding must have been stretched to the limits by my obsession and my constant use of the 'B' word.

Finally, I am especially grateful to The Crowood Press for having the courage and commitment to publish this book. Just like a Bantam, this book started first time and then ran and ran and ran.

The
BSA
BANTAM
IS
EVERYBODY'S
Motor Cycle !

B.S.A. CYCLES LTD., Birmingham 11

Printed in England

MC 158/40

Introduction

In the 1950s, BSA motorcycles were sold under the slogan 'BSA – The most popular motorcycle in the world'. It was no empty boast. Down in Armoury Road, Small Heath, Birmingham 11, the Birmingham Small Arms Company was making more motorcycles than all the other British manufacturers combined. Anyone who owned a 'Beesa' had a bike that was renowned, dependable, reliable, made to last and affordable. The range of machines on offer covered everything from small-capacity 'utilities' to full-blown 650cc twin-cylinder tourers and the all-conquering 350 and 500cc Gold Star singles. The most popular Beesa of them all did not have that kind of glamour, however. It was the smallest and the cheapest, and BSA's only successful two-stroke – the immortal Bantam.

The Bantam was minimalist, innocuous and sweetly simple. It involved the smallest number of moving parts that could carry a person at 40mph. It was easy to start and did not need a lot of looking after. Its unitary construction and lack of outside plumbing attracted customers who feared mechanical gadgets. All you had to do was open the fuel tap, half-close the air strangler – if it was cold – and tickle the carburettor until a squirt of fuel issued from a little hole in the float chamber. With one or maybe two steady follow-throughs on the kick-start lever, the egg-shaped engine would burst into life, making that distinctive 'ying-ber-bim-bim' sound as only a Bantam could. All that remained was to pull in the clutch lever, click the gear lever down into first and

The Birmingham Small Arms Company piled-arms motif was adopted in 1861 and was stamped, engraved or applied to every BSA product.

then, with a little practice, ease the clutch to engage a touch more throttle, and away it went. 'Oh, and don't forget to fully open the air strangler, Sir!'

A Bantam could be wheeled down an alleyway without scraping the walls, heaved up a kerb without causing a hernia and you did not need hob-nailed boots to kick-start it. Despite being a small bike it had big 19in diameter wheels 50½in (1250mm) apart and the saddle sat just 28in (70cm) from the ground. Beautifully proportioned, it was a pure and perfect example of functionality and purpose. It looked safe and it was

Opposite *Young and old, district nurses and students – everybody had a Bantam. (Courtesy Steve Foden, BSAOC)*

safe, with enough power for town and country, excellent handling and good brakes. Anyone could ride it; all you needed was a provisional licence and a pair of L-plates, and a few quid for a deposit on a hire purchase agreement.

In the glorious days of steam, the railway companies extolled the virtue of the streamlined pacific locomotive but they quietly made their fortune from little 0-6-0 engines that clanked on through the night. It was the same for BSA. The 500cc Gold Star singles embodied all that was good in engineering, style, speed and performance, yet it was that jack of all work, the everyman Bantam, that made the money in Birmingham.

The Bantam story touches every aspect and realm of motorcycling and has entered into motorcycling folklore. From L-plates to the racetrack, from two up with holiday luggage to scrambles and trials, a Bantam provided the necessary means to travel on nothing but pennies. In time, machines were bought and sold on, then changed hands again, and increasing numbers of people were brought their first taste of motorcycling freedom, adventure and a frugal way of going to work.

Bantams have been ridden in every corner of the world, from the snows of Mount Kilimanjaro back to the murky streets of industrial England. Never was there a motorcycle that gave such service yet was so abused, subjected to every mechanical torture and neglect. From the pretty little green, cream and gold showroom model to the last days of a pig-field runabout, a typical Bantam embodies fond memories of journeys past, the lingering pong of petroil, grease guns and oily chains, bulbs that blew and a sound that burbled and purred. Which Bantamite could forget that first moment of excitement when, for the first time, they took to the road? We loved them, we cursed them, but we all had a Bantam.

Below *From the 1920s through to the mid-1960s a BSA motorcycle really was that popular. The winged BSA motif was first adopted in 1943.*

Milestones

1861   Birmingham Small Arms company founded.

1910   First complete BSA motorcycle announced.

1928   BSA launch the 1.74 hp model A, their first two-stroke. German company Auto Union formed by amalgamation of DKW, Audi, Horch and Wanderer.

1936   BSA unilateral armament programme begins.

1938   BSA builds factory on Studley Road, Redditch, for BESA machine guns.

1939   DKW produces 125cc two-stroke RT125.

1943   BSA adopts winged 'B' motif and plans return to peacetime production.

1948   March: Lightweight 125cc two-stroke engine announced by BSA. Made at the Redditch factory.

        June: Model D1 lightweight 125cc two-stroke motorcycle announced (export only).

        October: Model D1 'Bantam' available in the UK. Competition D1 announced. Plunger-sprung frame option. De-Luxe Bantam with spring frame and Lucas electrics.

1951   May: 50,000th D1 comes off Small Heath assembly line.

1953   November: 100,000th D1 Bantam produced. Wico-Pacy introduces Series 55 Mk 8 generators. BSA Motorcycles Ltd and BSA Cycles Ltd formed as separate divisions.

1954   October: 148cc Model D3 Bantam Major announced. Competition models discontinued. S/A frame for D3 Bantam Major.

1956   Jack Sangster succeeds as Chairman of BSA. October. 175cc Model D5. Bantam Super announced, replaces D3 Major.

1957   February. 150,000th Bantam produced.

1958   BSA Owners Club formed in Sheffield. October: Model D7 Bantam Super announced replaces D5.

1963   Model D1 discontinued.

1965   D7 De Luxe introduced. Bantam engine assembly transferred to Small Heath.

1966   D7 Silver replaces D7 Super. July: D10 Bantams announced – Silver, Supreme, Sportsman and Bushman.

1967   October: D14/4 series – Supreme, Sportsman and Bushman.

1969   Bantam 175 or B175 models replace D14/4.

1970   Redditch factory closes.

1971   BSA company loses £8 million. All Bantam production ended.

1972   Further £3 million loss declared by BSA group.

1973   BSA absorbed into Manganese Bronze Holdings, Norton Villiers Triumph Company formed. BSA models no longer poduced.

1977   Small Heath factory demolished.

1 Fortunes of War

Origins

The BSA Bantam was as British as roast beef and red telephone boxes. In the old days, when policemen were paternal figures like Dixon of Dock Green and a £1 note was worth a fortune, the Bantam was ridden by anyone from a tweedy middle-aged lady pottering along a leafy lane to a factory worker making his way down a cobbled street on a cold grey morning. For the young lad making a reckless dash with the throttle wide open and L-plates flapping in the breeze, it was the first stepping-stone in a lifetime of motorcycling. Throughout the 1950s and 60s, the Bantam was an everyday feature of British life. It was safe, reliable and seemingly innocent.

The Birmingham Small Arms Company that built the Bantam had played a very significant role in the defeat of Nazi Germany and took the original design as reparation. The stark fact is that this humble little motorbike started as a leftover from the rubble and chaos of the Second World War. The design schemes had not come from drawing boards in Small Heath, Birmingham, but were once conceived in Germany by the DKW Company during the Hitler years and eventually brought to BSA.

Two-Strokes

During the inter-war years, small-capacity two-stroke engines struggled hard to gain acceptance in British motorcycling, being regarded as something of a novelty or a toy. However, the advantages of a power unit that fired on every downward stroke of the piston without the aid of mechanically operated valves were considerable, especially for a mode of transport where a high ratio of power to weight was essential. But the two-stroke was still primitive and power outputs very low. In the realms of small-capacity lightweight motorcycles, two-strokers were considered to be flimsy, finicky, frail and too erratic to be credible. A four-stroke single offered lusty torque, flexibility and a range of aesthetically pleasing engine architecture, graced with an exhaust note that sounded mellow, rose on a chromatic scale and could therefore be classified as music. A two-stroke by contrast looked bad and sounded ugly.

In Britain, if it was two-stroke, it was almost certainly from Villiers of Wolverhampton, the established manufacturer of small-capacity two-stroke engines that powered anything from Atco lawnmowers to pleasure boats. Following a road tax concession for motorcycles up to 150cc, effective from 1 January 1932, every small-time company hoping to get rich by making cheap 'tiddler' motorcycles ordered its engines from Villiers. It was a cut-throat business in which few would survive and the situation only added to the deep-rooted prejudice that two-stroke engines made too much noise without getting anywhere, belched clouds of blue smoke and were the lowest form of motorized life endured by riders who always stank of petrol.

BSA promoted a low-cost, mass-appeal machine powered by its own two-stroke engine. In 1928 the company announced a two-speed 174cc model 'A', but it was hopelessly underpowered and only a handful were ever sold. In 1939 there was an attempt to produce a small two-stroke autocycle, codenamed F10. While this acceptable-looking device pre-dated the post-war genus of Raleigh Wisps, NSU Quicklys and

A DKW RT125 as supplied to the German Army during the Second World War.

a BSA-built New Hudson autocycle, the outbreak of war effectively put paid to any chances of mass production.

On the continent, the attitude towards the lightweight two-stroke was very different. In France the Velo-Solex *bicyclettes à moteur* required no road tax and did not even need to be registered. The customer could simply walk into a shop, hand over a fistful of francs and ride home. In Germany the subject was far more serious. Concessions, inducements and a hardline policy against imports from abroad encouraged a determination to attain supremacy in many aspects of engineering especially if it had military potential.

Developments in Germany

In Saxony, the Zschopauer Motorradwerk was the home of DKW, founded by Danish engineer J.S. Rasmussen in 1919. The initials DKW are often thought to refer to *Das Kleine Wunder* ('the little miracle'), a nickname reflecting the company's involvement in the manufacture of small-capacity two-wheelers. However, at the start of the company's history, 'DKW' referred to an early product, the *Dampfkraftwagen* ('steam car').

In the early 1920s, the great German designer Hugo Ruppe created the first motorcycle to bear the company's initials. DKW went on to specialize in building two-stroke powered machinery, including a breed of racing machines that varied in size from 125cc to 600cc. At one time, the Zschopau factory was the largest motorcycle production unit in the world.

In 1932 DKW joined with three other Saxony motor manufacturers – Audi, Horch and Wanderer – to form Auto Union. (Their adopted four-ring trademark, signifying the merger of the companies, is still used today by Audi.) By 1939, DKW had the largest and most intensive racing department in the world, with about 150 men assigned to the task of dominating the racing circuit. Their tenacious desire for victory with a two-stroke led them to build up an unassailable high level of expertise. Their work was advanced and thorough, and sometimes pure genius. Superchargers, primary charging pistons and double piston designs running on alchohol produced engines that revved to unfathomable heights and produced an ear-splitting, high-pitched scream. The racing team at DKW built a 250cc engine producing 49bhp and a '350cc' producing nearly 60bhp, proving that a well-prepared two-stroke engine could come close to achieving a power ratio of 200bhp/ltr.

As well as being the home of the famous pre-war shrieking DKW, or 'Screaming Deek', the Zschopauer Motorradwerk also turned out thousands of cheap and simple motorcycles for regular consumption. One of these was a neat and compact 125cc lightweight model called the RT125 (*Reichstype* 125cc). In common with many German-engineered products of the late 1930s, the 1939 RT125 was robust and functional, with a cleverly disguised military capability. It was powered by a self-contained, unit-constructed 'power egg' with integral three-speed gearbox and flywheel magneto. Designed by Hermann Weber, the RT125 featured Schnuerle twin loop transfer ports and a light flat-top piston. For such a simple machine the little DKW was far ahead of anything known. It could propel itself and a laden (armed) rider at an unfazed 56km/h, go anywhere and consume just one litre of fuel for at least every 40km. It was no surprise that a re-equipped Wehrmacht spoiling for a war of rapid mobility acquired over 21,000 of these machines over the next few years.

Armaments Production

Despite the likelihood of another European conflict, the British Government led by Neville Chamberlain (a former BSA director) remained passive to Hitler's ranting and pursued a policy of appeasement. The view taken by the board of directors at the Birmingham Small Arms company was more realistic. Acting on a report submitted by one of its executives, James Leek, BSA began to produce stockpiles of weapons and munitions. The report, compiled after a visit to the 1936 Leipzig trade fair, had strongly urged an armaments programme with or without government orders. When war eventually came, in September 1939, BSA was able to supply the British Expeditionary Force.

BSA embarked on grand-scale production of Lee-Enfield rifles and Browning machine guns for Spitfire aircraft, but one particular weapon type prompted the building of a new factory that was to play an important part in BSA's later progress with a two-stroke motorcycle.

In 1937, the War Office was looking to re-equip the army with new tank-mounted medium and heavy machine guns. BSA had already been studying a type developed in Czechoslovakia, sending some weapons experts to the Zbrojovka works outside Brno to witness a demonstration of some prototype ZB 7.92mm and 15mm calibre guns. Similar in operation to the Bren-type weapon, the ZB guns were simple yet sturdy and able to give a high rate of sustained fire without having to change barrels. BSA negotiated an agreement to make the smaller-calibre gun under licence with an option to build the heavier type at a later date. Given the state of affairs in Europe, the BSA team smuggled half of the blueprints back to Birmingham, while the rest were delivered by Czech agents travelling by a different route.

Pressure on factory space at Small Heath was already at a premium when the Munich crisis of September 1938 hastened the need to increase the production capacity of a whole range of gun types. The company had to look elsewhere and plans to build a new factory on Studley Road in Redditch were given the go-ahead. (The Studley road factory should not to be confused with an earlier BSA Redditch factory in Lodge Road. BSA annexed this former Eadie Cycle Works building in 1909 and closed its doors for good in 1928 as the great depression began to bite.) Key production engineers were transferred from Birmingham and by 27 June 1939, barely a month before war erupted, the first BSA-produced 7.92mm gun was fired. The guns were modified at the Redditch factory and renamed 'BESA'. From a trickle of just a handful of guns at the outbreak of war, monthly production rose sharply to 200 in May 1940 to a peak of 2,600 by October 1942, as General Montgomery (later Field Marshal) was building up the Eighth Army behind El Alamein.

War Reparations and Peacetime Manufacturing

By August 1944 the BSA board of directors was already discussing a return to peacetime manufacturing as the Allied armies were advancing across Europe. Plans to start building a range of machines based on the 1940 civilian programme were already in operation. Boardroom minutes record the concerns voiced by James Leek, now BSA Managing Director, about the poor state of some of the models and the need to make a small-capacity model. Another item on the agenda concerned the receipt of a tender from a Swedish company for a consignment of small-capacity two-stroke engines intended for proprietary use. No further official details were given until February 1948 when a statement released by BSA announced that the company was indeed producing a batch of 123cc two-stroke engines to fulfil an overseas contract.

In a relatively short time, a company with no

The DKW RT125 as it appeared in 1939. It became the template for many post-war lightweight motorcycles the world over, including the BSA Bantam.

credible two-stroke experience had carried out a rapid development programme in unfamiliar technology in order to produce an efficient and advanced design. With skilled engineers and draughtsmen in short supply, it was no mean achievement. It transpired that help had come from an unlikely source.

The war reparations agreements hammered out by the Western Allies shared out the spoils from a defeated Germany. Anything from cameras to chemicals were effectively plundered and split between the victors. The DKW RT125 was just one item on a long list of hardware offered to British companies and any surviving legible drawings of the machine had been handed over to Villiers. Villiers showed little interest, declining the option, and the drawings were offered to BSA. One rumour suggests that members of the Parachute Regiment had arranged for the shipment home of a captured machine during 1944. Although there is no proof of any such action, a complete 123cc DKW machine was delivered to the newly established experimental department installed at Redditch in May 1946. Les Whittaker, the chief draughtsman assigned to the task of making something of it, was advised to keep quiet

and treat it as another hush-hush job relating to the war effort. In charge of the project was Mr Erling Poppe, a former designer of trucks and buses, who did have some sound motorcycle experience during the 1930s with his own exciting but ill-starred Packman and Poppe machine.

John Garner was one of those involved with Mr Poppe on a wide range of projects going on at Redditch behind closed doors. One of these was a 2-ltr flat-twin diesel lorry engine, another was a hand-operated truck mover for the railways, and then came the 125cc lightweight motorcycle job.

'The 123cc German DKW motorcycle was finished in matt black but had no badges on the tank,' according to Garner. 'The front forks were pressed steel and suspension used thick rubber bands. The engine had already been dismantled but it had a dynamo and coil ignition. The bike was hitched to a small open box sidecar made out of steel tube and aluminium panels. The raised front parapet had a lug; we all thought it was for mounting a gun!'

The Bantam Builders

The wartime generation that grew up on weak tea, Bovril and Spam knew what the initials BSA meant. It stood for 'Bloody Sore Arse' – just ask anyone who rode a khaki '500 Beesa' or served in the Transport Corp (although the officer class may have used the slightly less colourful 'Bum Sore Association'). Both euphemisms probably date from before the war but just about everyone who lived through the war years knew that BSA was the factory in Birmingham that made most of the British Army's motorbikes. The company also made hundreds of thousands of Lee Enfield rifles, machine guns, and massive amounts of bits, parts and other metal pieces that helped the Allied armies to win the war.

The Birmingham Small Arms company played its part during the Second World War as it had during the Great War of 1914–18, the Boer War of 1899–1901, and many other colonial squabbles of the old Empire days. Its history dates back to 1861 when a group of Birmingham gunsmiths clubbed together 'to make guns by machinery'. The gunsmiths had already forged themselves into an association during the Crimean War of 1852–55 in response to a Government-backed ordnance factory set up in Enfield. The newly formed BSA company built its factory in Small Heath on the eastern edge of Birmingham and over the next hundred years huge amounts of rifles were carted away from the factory gates up a throughfare called Armoury Road.

There was no profit in peacetime for a weapons maker. During periods of calm the company had to find other activities to keep its workers employed. The bicycle boom of the late Victorian era offered an ideal alternative. The machines that made shell cases also made very good wheel hubs and BSA soon earned a good reputation for making the finest cycle components as well as complete bikes. In 1880, a Mr E.C.F. Otto brought his weird and wonderful 'Dicycle' to Small Heath and demonstrated it to the directors by riding it on the boardroom table! Mr Otto then proceeded to take his amazing machine into the street and was last seen riding off towards the town at what was described as 'a reckless pace'. Throughout BSA's long association with two-wheeled contraptions, its bicycles all carried the famous BSA badge of three stacked rifles, officially known as the 'piled arms'.

BSA entered the world of motor-bicycle making in 1910 and produced a workmanlike 500 sidevalver for general sale in 1911. Other types and models followed and 'Beesa' motorbikes gained a reputation for value and reliability, with the quality people expected of products 'Made in England'.

The outbreak of war in 1914 saw BSA return to making huge amounts of Lee-Enfield Mark III rifles, Lewis machine guns, shells of all calibres, aero engines and the transmission to drive the first tanks. By the time of the armistice, BSA was an industrial giant that could count Daimler Cars in Coventry and Jessop-Saville special steels in Sheffield among its many assets.

During the inter-war years, BSA was re-established as the leading motorcycle manufacturer, and BSAs could be found everywhere in the world: someone had even ridden one to the top of Mount Snowdon! The company produced a wide range of machines, from 150cc Model XO 'tiddlers' to the sidecar-hauling 1000cc 'World Tour' V-twin, but it really made its name on the back of its low-cost 250cc models. They would never achieve any fame on the sports pages but they carried people to work day in, day out, without complaint.

continued on page 20

Above *Another day's production of 125cc D1 Bantam engines at Studley Road, Redditch, c. 1950. Early 'pineapple head' with Wico-Pacy Geni-mag electrics are evident. (Courtesy Alistair Cave)*

Right *The Birmingham Small Arms Company factory around 1959. The three-block West Building stood on the corner of the Golden Hillock Road and Armoury Road, Small Heath, Birmingham. It was originally built in 1915 to manufacture Lewis machine guns, exclusively supplied to the British Army by BSA during the Great War. The building was extensively damaged during the November 1940 blitz with great loss of life. (Courtesy Alistair Cave)*

continued from page 18

BSA had began to make and stockpile weapons long before the invasion of Poland in 1939. Most of this production was left wrecked on the beaches of Dunkirk and the colossal task of re-arming the country and her allies began. The company found itself in the front line. The large and sprawling Small Heath factory occupied a site where the Great Western Railway crossed the Grand Union Canal, making it an easy target. In November 1940, the main Small Heath factory fell victim to the Blitz and 53 employees were killed.

At the end of the Second World War, BSA was making anything from press tools for biscuit tins to Browning machine guns and employed a workforce of 28,000, based mainly at Small Heath but also at a number of satellite factories, including Studley Road, Redditch. The many subdivisions of the BSA empire included cars, radios, machine tools, coal washing and special steels. The scale of production during the war had been colossal. Six years of continuous round-the-clock shift work had produced over one million .303 calibre Lee-Enfield service rifles, 468,000 Browning machine guns at the rate of 10,000 per month, 400,000 Sten guns, 75,000 Hispano and Oerlikon cannons, as well as a billion or so components stamped with the piled-arms trademark. In addition, there were 126,000 500cc sidevalve M20 motorcycles, which came off the production line at a rate of one every four minutes and gave many a despatch rider a BSA!

During the following years and throughout the 1950s BSA motorcycles enjoyed a golden age with a succession of well-made, practical and popular models. Selling a range of machines, from the supremely successful 650cc A10 Golden Flash and the all-conquering Gold Star singles to the faithful Bantam, approved BSA dealers enjoyed brisk business. BSA company chairman Sir Bernard Docker and his wife Lady Norah indulged themselves in an opulent lifestyle, seriously at odds with a nation trying to graft its way out of lingering austerity. In 1956, the Dockers were ousted in one of the fiercest and most ill-tempered boardroom takeover battles in corporate history. The company continued to flourish but it was never quite the same again. Daimler was sold to Jaguar and BSA Cycles went to Raleigh as the core business became centred on motorcycles.

Machine shop No. 2, Studley Road, Redditch. Bantam alloy casings and covers by the score are being machined by piece-rate, vertical miller operators. (Courtesy Alistair Cave)

In the mid-1960s foreign competition had begun to attack BSA's domination and the company struggled to respond to the challenge, particularly in the lightweight motorcycle sector. The US market was a dominant factor in company policy, with 80 per cent of production intended for North American export. In 1967 and 1968, BSA was awarded the Queen's Award for Industry, but bad decisions, bungled planning and ill-conceived designs began to have an effect. By 1971 BSA had run up a trading deficit of £8.5 million. A restructured company under new management fought valiantly but could not halt the losses. Government intervention led to a takeover by Manganese-Bronze Holdings and the eventual formation of Norton-Villiers Triumph, a mere remnant of Britain's once-proud motorcycle industry leader. Plans to save Small Heath were thwarted and the era of the BSA motorcycle came to an end.

The plating shops at Small Heath were cold, dank and smelly. This is where all the chromium-plated parts for Bantams and other BSA models were prepared. (Courtesy Alistair Cave)

One of the machine shops at Redditch churning out thousands of engine and gearbox parts. (Courtesy Alistair Cave)

Developing and Testing the Prototype

Once the engine of the DKW motorcycle had been inspected, drawings were prepared and sufficient parts were ordered to make six complete engines, all in left-hand form, as on the original. Most parts were copied, but some were changed, including the clutch drum and crankshaft flywheels, which were made of steel instead of cast iron, as on the DKW model. Other modifications made room for a Lucas generator, an Amal carburettor and Whitworth threads.

After a session of high-speed bench testing, one of the BSA engines was placed into the DKW frame and sent out for road testing. During the first tests, the crankshaft drive sprocket key sheared and the clutch centre seized on its shaft. A wider key and a bronze bush for the clutch soon rectified the trouble. The prototype was then ridden to the Bwlch-Y-Groes mountain pass in deepest Wales for some lengthy endurance testing with John Garner at the controls.

'I was 14 stone, 5ft 11in tall and just eighteen years old at the time,' recalls Garner. 'I made three climbs up the Bwlch and the piston tightened up a few times. Back at Redditch the piston was found to be scored and the second ring stuck in its groove but the engine had kept going.'

The only other problem occurred on the outward journey and was not attributed to the engine. 'The petrol tank had been welded up, causing some flaking inside and some of it kept getting into the carburettor,' says John Garner. 'I had to keep stripping the carb to get the bike running again. Mr Poppe and his party came along and when I told him of my trouble he took the filler cap off and manhandled the bike upside down, emptying out the petrol. He then personally supervised the flushing out of the tank and mixed a new tankful of petrol and oil himself!'

After more testing it was found that the German-made Bing carburettor performed much better than the British-made Amal. On full throttle the test bike was doing 52mph (83km/h) against 49mph (78.5km/h) with the rider in a sitting-up position. Fuel consumption also favoured the Bing, with a return of over 140mpg (2ltr/100km) as opposed to 128mpg (2.2ltr/100km) at a steady 30mph (45km/h). With these figures in mind, BSA ordered a set of die tools to make copies of the Bing but then the project went back to the drawing board to redesign the engine into a mirror image, placing the gear-shift and kick-starter on the right-hand side for the British market. Commercial considerations won the day. Instead of Lucas electrics and Bing carburation, a Wico-Pacy Geni-mag flywheel magneto was specified, along with an Amal carburettor.

The DKW RT125 became the most frequently copied machine in motorcycling history, and not just by Western Allies. The very first powered two-wheeler produced by Japanese piano maker Yamaha was an almost exact duplicate of the RT125 and nowhere as discreet as the BSA version. The Russian Mockba M1A and a Polish WSK could both be traced back to the same blueprints. American manufacturer Harley-Davidson called its version the Hummer and it stayed in production until 1966. Even in a country obsessed with big horsepower, it seems there was still room for an economy lightweight. The copies everywhere were so accurate that an engine taken from any version would fit any

other frame. It was even reputed that parts from the Russian and Polish models could be interchanged both with each other and with the original DKW!

Post-War Years at BSA

The immediate post-war era at BSA was a time for the rebuilding and consolidation of its domination of the UK motorcycle market. Many of the machines produced in 1945 were essentially the same as those in the pre-war range but with telescopic forks. In 1946 the 500cc A7 twin was introduced, becoming, along with the later 650cc A10 Golden Flash, the all-time classic that saw BSA's motorcycles division go from strength to strength. A new 125cc lightweight model would be a worthy addition to the range. Prototype building and testing of a complete lightweight motorcycle with a BSA-designed and manufacture had advanced throughout 1947. In March 1948, the company issued a press release in the guise of a contract supplied, announcing an all-enclosed 123cc two-stroke engine.

A motorcycle yet to have a name. This rare picture of the 1947 prototype BSA 125cc two-stroke shows many interesting features. The primary chaincase has an inspection cap and the rear mudguard lacks any worthwhile protection. The carburettor is probably a German Bing and the front forks have no gaiters. The bulb horn, fuel tank and rectangular toolbox with two fasteners would later appear on the first Bantam production models. The exhaust is from a 'C'-range 250cc OHV model. BSA had yet to learn some of the fundamentals of building two-strokes. (Courtesy Steve Foden, BSAOC)

The announcement described a unit-constructed engine producing a modest 4bhp at 5,000rpm. It used a plain, dome-topped, Lo-ex alloy piston and a Schnuerle twin loop scavenging system, which certainly stoked up some interest in engineering circles. The design was against accepted British conventions, with a primary drive taken on the right-hand side using a non-adjustable chain held on close centres of clutch and drive sprocket. A cast-iron cylinder barrel, raked forwards on its crankcase, was capped with an alloy cylinder head and held down on to the crankcase by four long studs. At the time, most engines still used flange-mounted cylinder barrels bolted to the crankcases. Full circular balanced flywheels and a crankshaft supported on three well-proportioned ball bearings – two on the drive side and one on the opposite flank – were the key features that were to be responsible for the engine's renowned longevity and resilience.

Inside BSA's tidy, compact unit with its egg-shaped casing was a positive-stop, three-speed gear cluster and a roller-type big-end bearing. On the nearside, a Wico-Pacy magneto generator had a heavy permanent magnet rotor flywheel keyed and locked to the crankshaft. Over on the drive side, the clutch was beautifully light to operate and ingeniously simple, with a quick-action helix mechanism that worked a pushrod running through the gearbox mainshaft. Strangest of all was the kick-start and foot-operated gear levers fixed on a concentric shaft axis. The length and position of the levers relative to the footrest meant that riders had to adopt certain habits. The kick-start was operated with the instep rather than the heel and gear changes in motion were made by moving the right leg completely off the footpeg. With an Amal 261 carburettor, with built-in air filter and strangler attached to the cylinder barrel by spigot and clip, the complete engine unit needed just four mounting bolts and weighed only 45lb.

Simplicity: exploded details of an early D1 'pineapple head' engine with Wipac Geni-mag electrics.

Doctor Schnuerle's Magic Loop

As long as the Bantam owner opened the fuel tap, closed the air strangler (if it was cold) and applied two or three kicks, the engine would burst into life with its unique sound. Clicking down into first gear, and applying a steady but gentle opening of the throttle, while gradually letting loose the clutch lever, man and machine would set off down the road.

Bantam riders were being propelled by a fairly sophisticated piece of thermodynamic technology, the result of many years of hard development and brainwork on an engine that was simple, and imperfect.

The two-stroke internal combustion engine dates back to Victorian times. Mr (later Sir) Dugald Clerk's patented high-speed gas engine provided combustion every time the piston reached the top of its travel. It used an external charging cylinder and cam-operated valves – not quite what might be expected of a two-stroke engine. The matter was somewhat improved by Joseph Day's two-port or three-port engines of 1891, which cunningly used the piston for both pumping and compressing the fuel/air mixture. Simultaneous events took place when the piston commenced both its upward and downward stroke. As fuel vapour and air were mixed in a carburettor, a rising piston drew the mixture into the crankcase. As the piston began a downward stroke, the mixture was pumped upward through a transfer pipe and fed back into the cylinder above the piston, which was by now starting its upward movement. This time, as the piston moved upwards, it blocked off the transfer port and compressed the mixture. As it reached top dead centre, ignition took place, forcing the piston rapidly back down and uncovering an exhaust port to allow the spent gases to escape. With luck, the crankshaft, cogs and wheels would then go happily around.

continued overleaf

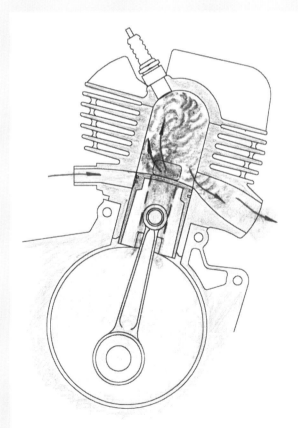
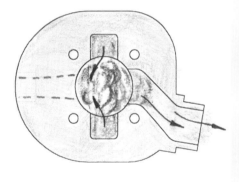

The Schnuerle twin loop scavenging system gave the BSA Bantam an efficient two-stroke engine.

continued from page 25

Unlike the four-stroke Otto cycle, which only fired every other time the piston reached top dead centre, the two-stroke used no valves. It promised engines that were lighter and cheaper to produce and a powerplant that could be twice as powerful as a four-stroke, in theory at least.

The challenge to all engineers was how to get all the puffing and blowing in the right sequence and at the right time. To solve the problem of stopping a fresh supply of fuel and air from shooting across the top of the piston, going down the exhaust port and into the street, Mr Day's engine relied upon a gas-tight crankcase and a deflector, a strange horn-shaped projection cast on to the top of the piston. The deflector method worked but was not very efficient in separating a fresh in-going charge from the combusted gasses trying to get out. Many two-stroke engines used in small motor-boats and motorcycles used this device with acceptable results but the two-

stroke engine sadly lagged behind its four-stroke counterpart when it came to delivering what all motorcyclists craved – a feeling of power, stomp and guts when the throttle was twisted.

In the struggle to find the Holy Grail – perfect combustion without mechanically operated valves – various attempts were made to improve the Day engine, involving additional piston chambers and other pumping gadgets. They all foundered or proved to be self-defeating. During the 1920s a number of German engineers doggedly carried on with the development of two-stroke internal combustion engine. One of the most significant improvements was the Schnuerle loop transfer system. Dr Schneurle was a senior development engineer with DKW in the late 1920s. In his engine, the fuel/air mixture was fed from the crankcase by two opposing transfer ports placed on either side of the piston. The size, direction and shape of the transfer ports, together with

continued on page 28

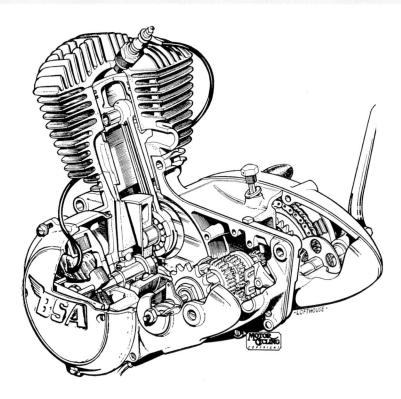

Engine cut-away of the 1954 large-fin barrel engine.

Right *The Bantam engine was a self-contained power unit. Note the concentric kick-start and gear-change levers. The large finned barrel and head style appeared in 1954. (Owen Wright)*

Below *As explained in 1961, as every schoolboy should know. Simple, isn't it? (Courtesy Steve Foden, BSAOC)*

This is how the BSA Bantam works!

Like all petrol engines it works by the pressure of hot gas. This pushes the piston down and causes the crankshaft to rotate. A chain on the crankshaft drives the gearbox and another chain from the gearbox drives the rear wheel. Simple isn't it?

The hot gas comes from the burning of a mixture of petrol vapour and air which is supplied by the carburetter, and which goes into the crankcase first. When the piston comes down it pushes it from the crankcase through transfer ports into the cylinder. The piston then comes up and compresses it, a spark at the plug starts it burning, and down goes the piston on another power stroke.

The Bantam engine is a two-stroke which means that every downward stroke of the piston is a power stroke. Every time the exhaust goes "pop" the crankshaft has revolved once so you can imagine how fast the engine is revolving when you hear the smooth purr of a Bantam as it passes by.

SPARKING PLUG

CYLINDER HEAD

CYLINDER BARREL

PISTON

CARBURETTER

EXHAUST

CONNECTING ROD

CRANK ASSEMBLY

continued from page 26

the shape of the combustion space, gave the incoming charge a tendency to swirl around for an instant, while the combusted gases made a quick exit. It meant that the piston could be simpler, more lightweight and have a plain or slightly domed crown, without needing the peculiar deflectors found on other engines. A later advance positioned two transfer ports opposite each other, roughly at right-angles to the inlet and exhaust tracts. This system, correctly known as twin-loop scavenging, was adopted on most small two-stroke motorbikes, including the BSA Bantam.

Having a constant whiff of petrol vapour into the crankcase every time the flywheel turned was not an ideal way to treat the main supporting ball bearings or a piston blazing up and down the cylinder. The precious working parts, if they were to last for any appreciable amount of time, needed a regular and efficient supply of oil. With no cost-effective way of force-feeding oil into the engine bottom end (the cost and complexities of an auxiliary pump would have been self-defeating), the answer was to simply put the oil into the petrol. Under pressure inside the crankcase, the two ingredients would separate out, leaving the petrol to burn in the cylinder head and the oil to deposit itself on all the moving parts. Of course, it was not as straightforward as that and certainly not 100 per cent efficient. Some of the oil also got burnt, which meant that Bantam owners left a faintly blue haze in their wake and had to spend odd weekends scraping and unclogging the engine of oily gunge and encrusted carbon. Such was the tolerant nature of the Bantam that over 100,000 D1 models ran with petroil-lubricated main bearings, clocking up very high mileages, before modifications ensured a positive oil feed from the gearbox oil.

The D1

On 24 June 1948 a surprise press release was issued announcing a completely new motorcycle 'for export only'. It was designated as the light-weight model D1. The 125cc engine was now slung into an all-welded frame with a rigid rear-wheel support and non-hydraulic telescopic forks. With generous 19in tyres on a 50in (1250mm) wheelbase, and 5in (12.5cm) diameter half-width hub brakes back and front, it looked both safe and stable. Features included a spring-up centre stand, rear carrier, rectangular toolbox and adjustable handlebars. The lighting switchgear was contained within the headlamp shell and controlled by a Bowden cable lever mounted on the handlebar, probably the most complicated part on the whole bike. One idea borrowed from the DKW was the way in which the clutch and front brake lever brackets were welded directly to the handlebars. It all added up to a clean and uncluttered control layout.

The mudguards were amply valanced; the rear-guard side valancing was tapered towards the rear in the old pre-war style. The front guard was wide enough to carry the registration number on either flank and, fastened to fixed fork tubes, it did not reciprocate with the movement of the wheel or add to the unsprung weight. Even the sprung saddle, either a Mansfield or a Wrights, was far better than the primeval rubber seats that riders had previously endured.

The D1 was finished in an all-over light green, with cream panels on the fuel tank sides and lined in dark red and gold. The shade was sometimes called Pastel Green, or, more often, Mist Green, and it represented a welcome splash of colour in an otherwise drab world. For a machine that was devoid of any bright plating and had an exhaust silencer shaped like a duck's bill, the D1 was the prettiest yet.

Reports and accounts of the very earliest 1948 models suggest that the first people to stake a down payment were impressed by a tenacious little bike that was forgiving, easy to ride and a joy for novices. It had a slow-revving engine that could be pulled from low speed without snatch, had boundless energy, was easy to start and thrived on hard work. The best features of the D1 – easy controls with a light action, effective brakes and nimble handling – were embodied from the very start. And anyone who ever ventured out on a D1 would remember the rubber bulb horn that was cleverly mounted through the steering head-

Opposite *The small machine with a big future. The Bantam as it appeared in 1949. (Courtesy Steve Foden, BSAOC)*

THESE FEATURES ENSURE TROUBLE-FREE RELIABILITY

B.S.A. "Bantam" 125 c.c.

View of deflectorless piston head with combustion chamber machined all over for consistent efficiency.

The robust flywheel assembly with "faced" flywheels to ensure minimum air friction and maximum induction-transfer efficiency.

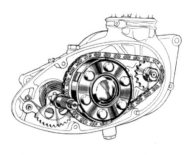

Unit construction of engine and gearbox with totally enclosed primary drive and kickstarter mechanism.

Tot
mag
con

extra low petrol consumption

The new B.S.A. "Bantam" 125 c.c. will undoubtedly prove extremely popular, because it gives all the advantages of motor cycling — delightful, easy, speedy transport — in its most economical form.

The two-stroke engine has a really amazing reserve of power — the machine will cruise indefinitely at 40 m.p.h. — and is exceptionally flexible.

It is light and easy to handle, holds the road perfectly at all speeds, and is — as you can be confident any B.S.A. product will be — completely reliable.

sed combined flywheel dynamo with built-in ker.

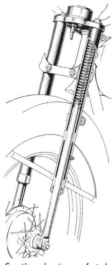

Sectional view of telescopic forks showing the long "easy" springs for comfort on all road surfaces.

stock; who could resist a quick 'parp' now and again? BSA took out a patent for it and it remained an endearing part of this characterful bike well into the early 1960s.

By October, the initial batch of production models had done enough miles to satisfy the engineers that the bike was reliable and proven. As a few machines started to be released on to the home market, the lightweight D1 acquired a name – 'Bantam', inspired by that small domestic fowl, of which the cock is a spirited fighter. This was not the first time that the name had been used for a motor vehicle. In 1933, the Bristol-based Douglas company had offered a 148cc two-stroke 'Bantam', but this was soon changed to 'Model X' in line with the fashion for describing 150s of the low taxation class. Singer used the name for its light motor car of 1935–37, but few would have known about that, or remembered it. Over the next few years, the name 'Bantam' became inextricably linked with BSA and with motorbikes in general.

The first published road test appeared in *The Motorcycle* on 28 October 1948. At the time the new D1 was still officially designated 'export only' and the report was thought something of a scoop. The 'blue 'un' gave a bright account of BSA's fighting cock. It was a cinch to ride, performance around town was brisk and fuel consumption worked out at a measly 128mpg (2.2ltr/100km). The motor was impossible to overdrive, and brakes and handling were quoted as being as 'safe as the Bank of England'. Its clean lines and easy maintenance made for an ideal economy motorcycle.

Pricing the Bantam at £60 plus purchase tax, BSA were on to a winner from the start. Although it was a compulsory fitting, the Smiths D-shaped speedometer was listed as an extra £3 3s 6d, and road tax for a '125' in 1948 was 17s 6d. Along with other such items such as number plates, the ready-for–the-road cost of buying a Bantam was therefore about £80. The very

When launched in 1948, the model D1 offered a clean, simple, easy-to-maintain design. (Courtesy Steve Foden BSAOC)

early export models had a winged BSA motif picked out in maroon characters applied to the cream tank panels. Now that the bike was identified officially as the Model D1 Bantam, the tank carried the proud and colourful 'BSA Bantam' cockerel transfers. It became as strong a brand image as the Michelin man and the Oxo cube.

How a plunger-sprung Lucas electric D1 Bantam De-Luxe appeared in Motor-Cycling *in February 1950.*

On the early models, the drive side cover did not have the later raised stripe with BSA lettering and the exhaust pipe passed in a rather ungainly fashion beneath the footrest. The centre stand was soon improved, with a deficient clip being replaced by a C-shaped arm and tension spring to give a better and more assured over-centre action. Performance for the early bird was recorded at 21, 41 and 47mph (33.5, 65.5 and 75km/h) in each gear, 0 to 30mph (45km/h) through the gears in 6.6 seconds, and a minimum

The 123 c.c.
Model DI

B.S.A.
"BANTAM"

A Spring-frame-equipped Edition of a Famous Two-stroke Fitted With Rectified A.C. Lighting

Although an ultra-lightweight, the B.S.A. "Bantam" accommodates a six-foot rider in comfort. Note the extensive mudguard valancing fore and aft.

(Right) This offside view of the machine emphasizes its attractive lines. On the streamlined crank-case-gearbox housing will be seen the gear-change and kick-starter pedals operating on a common axis.

Men at work: the Bantam engine assembly track at Redditch in around 1950. (Courtesy Alistair Cave)

non-snatch speed in top gear was 12mph (19km/h). With the roads and traffic the way they were in the late 1940s, a four-horse Bantam was a nippy and efficient way of getting about.

Exports to the Commonwealth

The post-war Attlee Labour government had been swept in on a landslide in the 1945 'khaki election' but celebrations were short-lived as US President, Harry S. Truman put an end to the lease-lend agreement, so that no goods could be obtained without a down payment. The resulting austerity measures were more severe than at any time during the war. Britain was virtually bankrupt. Manufactured goods were strictly consigned for export only, so the first batches of Bantams were shipped to all parts of the British Commonwealth. From Malayan rubber plantations to the vast expanses of colonial Africa and the sheep stations of Australia, the Bantam gained immediate respect. The Aussies were the first to start experimenting with the engine and, once its

wings had been unclipped with simple tuning and improvement, the plucky little green Beesa turned out to be a real flyer.

Redditch and Small Heath

Although Studley Road, originally built for making BESA machine guns, now had a Bantam engine assembly line in full swing, the Redditch plant became more synonymous with the Sunbeam S7, the 'gentleman's motorcycle', launched in mid-1946. BSA had bought the Sunbeam name from Associated Motorcycles (the Matchless-AJS people) during the war. Designed by Mr Erling Poppe, the Sunbeam was intended as a luxury tourer with a 500cc twin-cylinder in-line OHC engine that borrowed heavily from the car industry. Its wheels carried big balloon tyres and the engine drove the back wheel through a shaft drive. The Sunbeam S7 and later S8 were expensive and lacklustre when pitted against the fast and vivid parallel twin-cylinder machines coming from Triumph, Norton and Matchless-AJS, as well as BSA itself. Built on the assembly track adjacent to the line where Bantam engines were being pieced together, the Sunbeam was painted in the same Mist Green livery applied to the D1s. Too expensive and lacking guts, the Sunbeam lasted only until 1958. (Poppe had parted company with BSA in mid-1947.)

The Redditch plant had extensive machine shops, foundries for both ferrous and non-ferrous castings, and numerous assembly lines for producing stationary engines and other industrial equipment. The Bantam engine assembly track was a male-only reserve; in those days, the building of engines was considered to be a job only for able-bodied men. The track consisted of two rows of men facing each other, each one carrying out a single assembly task before sliding the holding fixture to the next man until the engine was a finished self-contained power unit. In its long and glorious heyday, the Bantam engine

The Bantam ladies at work, Small Heath, circa 1950. The most popular motorcycle in the world was built at the rate of 90 per day. (Courtesy Alistair Cave)

track produced between 90 and 125 units every day.

Batches of finished engines were inspected and number-stamped, then loaded on to a wagon and carted off to Small Heath, to the bosom of the BSA empire. There, where the workplace had wooden flooring and Victorian arched windows, the Bantam assembly line went into full flight. All the work, from lacing wheels to frame assembly, cabling and wiring, was carried out entirely by women, although they did borrow a man from time to time to sling the engines into place.

Women started to occupy the Small Heath workplace during the First World War as the strain on manpower increased. Machining and repetition tasks soon became part of a woman's work. Long before the days of human resource psychologists, the production bosses at BSA recognized that women possessed a high level of manual dexterity. Men undertaking repetitive tasks were less consistent and tended to cut corners. A woman seemed to be more likely to spend her working life performing the same repetitive job – on half the pay – without deviating from instructions, and to accept it all as part and parcel of life. The young women working on the assembly line would talk among themselves and keep going, whereas a group of blokes was more likely to down tools in order to dissect another dismal result for Birmingham City F.C.

Manufacturing and Testing

The Bantam was mass-manufactured following concepts and procedures made famous by Henry Ford. Banks of press tools punched out mountains of tank panels and mudguards. Shift-working and piece-rate lathe and cylindrical grinder operators continued day and night, churning out turned components such as wheel spindles and rough-cut gearbox parts. All assembly work was performed by hand. Manually operated presses assembled ball bearings into crankcases and wheel hubs but all finished machined and painted parts were knocked together with no more than basic

An early rigid model D1 Bantam polished for display in the BSA factory showroom circa 1950. (Courtesy BSA Owners Club)

hand tools and busy fingers.

Each and every finished Bantam was given a half-mile run around a test track. The job of riding 90 Bantams every day was shared between two 'road testers'. One was a young lad called Chris Vincent, who started as a fifteen-year-old at BSA and would go on to achieve greater things. Few Bantam owners knew that their pride and joy had first been ridden by a man who would later win a full international Sidecar TT for BSA in 1961 and also ride the rocket-firing 650cc A65 in the 1965 James Bond film *Thunderball*. Some of Vincent's later work with Bantams involved 10,000-mile endurance testing on the MIRA circuit at Nuneaton.

Testing and development often involved some ridiculous concepts. One idea that was briefly pursued was the fitting of a cast-iron piston. After testing, it was not taken up.

Earls Court Show 1948

In the years after the end of the war, there was an exciting resurgence in British design and manufacturing. Some concepts were destined for success, while others fell by the wayside. The Bristol Brabazon airliner was overweight and underpowered, while the de Havilland Comet, the first commercial jet-airliner, was brilliant but ultimately doomed. On the other hand, the Morris Minor, the first British car with monocoque construction, was massively popular, and the Land Rover, intended as a post-war stop-gap, is still going strong. Added to these was the BSA Bantam.

For the first time in ten years there was a British motorcycle show, held at London's Earls Court in November 1948. It broke all attendance records, with 130,000 paying visitors and 29 British manufacturers represented at the show with everything and anything for the enthusiast. Not all motorcycles on display were re-vamped editions of pre-war designs. There was more than a hint that a renaissance was taking place in British manufacturing. Velocette showed its technically interesting 149cc water-cooled OHV flat-twin LE; Triumph offered its unique 'sprung hub' across a range of sleek and speedy OHV twins; and Vincent-HRD stole the headlines with a high-performance 1000cc OHV V-twin Black Shadow.

During the post-war period of economic recovery people had worked long hours and saved money but as yet they had little to spend it on. As export restrictions began to be relaxed, ex-soldiers still clutching their de-mob gratuity were at last presented with the opportunity to buy a brand-new motorcycle. The visitors to Earls Court may have gaped, wished and prayed for a Norton Dominator, a Triumph Speed twin or the Vincent V-twin, but for most the reality was likely to be the 125cc Bantam, being shown in public for the first time.

2   BSA's Little Miracle (The D1 and D3 Models)

Earls Court 1949

'We have got something to shout about today,' pronounced a fresh-faced James Callaghan, MP and Parliamentary Secretary to the Ministry of Transport. 'Here is an industry in which Britain is "cock of the walk".' With that, the 1949 Earls Court motorcycle show was duly opened. The future Prime Minister might well have been referring to the BSA Bantam, which, just one year after its launch, was already a roaring success.

The model D1 Bantam was a little gem and by May 1951, BSA had made and sold 50,000 of them. In November 1953, after barely four years in production, the 100,000th Bantam was the centrepiece of the annual motorcycle show; it

was a world record for motorcycle production. A nationwide dealer network was constantly fighting for a better allocation and selling every bike they could manage. Sales had extended to 27 countries worldwide, although the vast majority of machines stayed in their home country. Both BSA and their thousands of Bantam customers

Opposite *The US market was one area that never achieved a successful sales record for the Bantam. (Courtesy Steve Foden, BSAOC)*

Below *The D1 Competition model as catalogued in 1950. This model, specifically aimed at trials eventing, had cylinder decompression, folding kick-start, large rear sprocket and roller bearing front axle amongst its features. (Owen Wright)*

BSA "BANTAM"

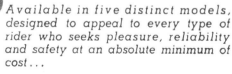

for 1950

Here's a machine specifically engineered to satisfy the needs of the sport enthusiast... The novice, as well as the seasoned expert, will find the performance superb in all kinds of going...

The "Bantam" — BSA's ruggedly constructed 125 cc motorcycle is equally as thrilling to operate on the super highway as on the long forgotten backwoods trail...

Available in five distinct models, designed to appeal to every type of rider who seeks pleasure, reliability and safety at an absolute minimum of cost...

STANDARD	STANDARD	COMPETITION	COMPETITION	DeLUXE SPRINGER
Rigid Frame "Bantam"	Springer "Bantam"	Rigid Frame "Bantam"	Spring Frame "Bantam"	Described below Lucas Equipped
$280.66	$299.50	$309.50	$329.50	$339.46

The World's foremost 125 cc Motorcycle has these outstanding features: Front and rear springing ... Generator and Battery lighting ... Sealed beam headlight . . Coil ignition... Rugged 5 horsepower engine ... New center stand ... Beautiful green finish with special 1950 "Bantam" tank insignia.

"SOMETHING TO CROW ABOUT"

1950 RETAIL PRICES inclusive of Fed. Tax, FOB New York and Los Angeles.

(Not inclusive of freight, set up charge or local taxes if any)

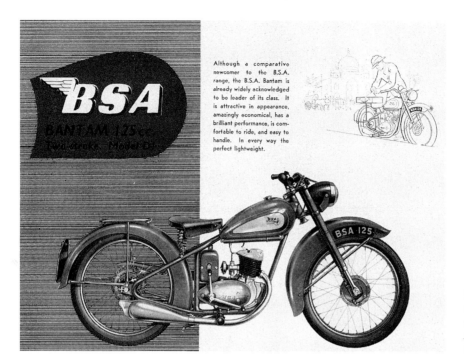

Although a comparative newcomer to the B.S.A. range, the B.S.A. Bantam is already widely acknowledged to be leader of its class. It is attractive in appearance, amazingly economical, has a brilliant performance, is comfortable to ride, and easy to handle. In every way the perfect lightweight.

Simplicity and functionality: the 1949 D1 with a rigid rear wheel and 'flat Bantam' silencer. (Courtesy Alistair Cave)

soon realized the incredible durability and stamina of the little bike. Unlike other contempory engines that used bob-weights, the balanced flywheel crankshaft did not pulverize its mainshaft bearings. Even the pre-1954 engine, which relied entirely on petroil lubrication, was capable of notching up very high mileages. During these formative years the Bantam became everyone's motorcycle, with a reputation and name that became part of the fabric of everyday life.

One particular Bantam at the 1949 show caused something of a stir in the sporting world, especially among those who had already recognized the Bantam's potential. Introduced to meet a significant demand for cheap weekend trials bikes, the Competition D1 had a decompressor fitted into the cylinder head, and the exhaust was raked upwards, with the now-familiar 'flat Bantam' silencer hung on the end. Unvalanced mudguards, a folding kick-start lever and a large wheel sprocket made it viable for the increasingly popular off-road sports. Riders soon discovered that it did not take much technical know-how to make a Bantam really go on a road circuit, and the

often overlooked story of the Bantam's sporting success began. (For more on making a Bantam go faster, see Chapter 5.)

Early Owners

Tom Scott was one of the first to buy a BSA Bantam. In March 1949 he saw a small green motorcycle in a showroom window. He had never seen anything like it before. It looked less complicated than the usual run-of-the-mill motorbike, uncluttered by complicated levers and oily pipes. It had modern telescopic front forks and was finished in willowy green with a splash of cream on the fuel tank. It looked neat and simple, not too small and certainly not too large. It was exactly what Tom wanted to escape the daily drudgery of bicycling or bussing to work. The 'BSA Bantam' badges on the tank meant that it must be worth having, so Tom went into the showroom and bought it.

Tom Scott's reasoning was typical of the time. His new bike was the first to be sold in his hometown of Morpeth, Northumberland. With purchase tax and a few other things to get going on the road, the total bill came to just £83. He rode it south to the Midlands to find work. A skilled pattern maker, he set up home in Rugby, Warwickshire, and the Bantam provided faithful daily service for the 25-mile round trip for the next 15 years – including coming home at mid-day for his dinner.

Petrol rationing officially ended in 1950. Motorists tore up their coupons in celebration and the motor trade predicted a sales boom. For most ordinary working people with more modest aspirations, the Bantam remained cheap and available. Throughout the 1950s, little green Bantams took to Britain's road, ridden by young and old, men and women. Bantam clubs and dedicated rider groups sprang up and 'Bantam' became a generic term for a lightweight motorcycle. The General Post Office placed large orders for its telegram delivery service, had them painted red and unleashed swarms of keen 16-year-old rid-

ers. Area gas boards used them for meter reading; the Forestry Commission found them ideal for getting about its terrain; and the army took a batch for internal camp transport. The Bantam became Britain's most familiar motorcycle, known even to those with only the slightest interest in motorcycling.

Denys Bryant began a five-year apprenticeship with the Southwest Electricity Board in 1952. From his home near Helston in Cornwall it was a 15-mile trip to work, passing by the RAF airfield at Culdrose, and his only form of transport was a Hercules bicycle. He paid a visit to C.G. Lory Ltd, the local dealership for Austin cars and BSA Motorcycles, and in March 1953, with a spot of help from his parent's savings, he became the proud owner of PRL 549. It was a latest series

Denys Bryant on his newly acquired 1953 D1 Lucas De-Luxe Bantam. (Courtesy Denys Bryant)

In the early 1950s, Buckinghamshire Constabulary patrolled the streets on D1 Bantams. (Courtesy Steve Foden, BSAOC)

125cc BSA Bantam with a sprung frame and Lucas lighting equipment. The ready-for-the-road price came to £108 9s 1d, including purchase tax (£22 10s), matching green legshields (£1 14s 6d), handlebar screen (£2 2s), road licence (13s 10d), petrol and oil (5s 6d) and a pair of tie-on L-plates (3s 3d).

In just over two years, Denys Bryant's Bantam covered 35,000 miles (55,000km) and never failed to return less than 120 miles per gallon. In true Bantamite tradition, the rider adopted the usual garb of a large rubber-lined canvas coat with press studs that also fastened between the legs, a pair of thick leather gauntlets and a black 'Corker' helmet with 'Skulgard' peak. Fortunately, the head protection was never put to the test, even on the one and only occasion when the Bantam went down on some ice. After he eventually passed his test, Bryant traded in the trusty D1 for a 250cc Beesa, getting a payback of £67 for the Bantam. The D1 had been well looked after. True to the instruction book, regular maintenance had been performed with liberal use of the grease gun and a periodic de-coke. The chain had been soaked in paraffin, cleaned and immersed in warmed-up graphite grease, and it was still in fine condition when the bike was sold. The only problem was a crack that started to appear in the upper steering yoke when the machine was still under warranty. It was replaced without question by the dealer. On another occasion, the lights also shorted out when the bike hit some floodwater.

Add-ons and accessories soon became available. For owners of the early D1, a dual seat proved to be the most welcome comfort improvement. Denys Bryant had one fitted almost immediately. It not only made the 15-mile trek to work less numbing it also attracted a long line of pillion 'friends', male and female.

After only a few weeks of riding, Denys Bryant was pulled up by a police motorcyclist who pointed out that the registration plates were not standard. The law stated that the painted characters should be all of the same thickness. Bryant was allowed to proceed on his way, provided he promised to correct the plates as soon as possible, and the policeman assured him that he would be speaking to the dealer about it, too. The Devon and Cornwall Constabulary really knew how to deal with a crime wave in those days.

L-Plates and Baling String

In the 1950s, the first motorcycle was for many young people the most exciting milestone on the road to adulthood, rather like getting served a pint in the pub. The question 'Can I have a motorbike?' would cause parents huge anxiety, but the locker rooms of the apprentice miners, engineers and railway workers were full of proud young things who bragged about a newly acquired machine; more often than not, it was the concerned parents who had stood as guarantors of some dodgy HP deal.

A BSA Bantam was a first bike for many thousands of youngsters and L-plates and a Bantam went together like bangers 'n' mash. A generation of young men with 30 bobs' worth of third-party insurance in their back pocket eagerly watched their first pride and joy – a second-hand, worse-for-wear Bantam bought 'on the knock' – wheeled from a dealer's lot to the kerbside. 'Training' was often rudimentary: 'That's the clutch, there's yer brakes, gears are one down, two up, off yer go. Oh and don't forget to put some oil in yer petrol.'

Practice took place in driveways, back alleyways and farmyards and the thrill of firing up the motor was tempered by the pain of the grazed elbows, skinned knees and damaged pride. With L-plates tied on with baling string or sticky tape, novices would spend half an hour kicking the engine over before realizing that the fuel tap was still closed. After the rider had got the throttle and clutch to work in harmony, and mastered a peculiar gear change action that required a lift of the complete limb rather than a deft flick of a toe cap, the bike would lurch forwards at what seemed like warp speed. According to H.C. Haycraft in *The Book of the BSA Bantam*, 'If it is your first run on a motor-cycle, you will doubtless now seem to be travelling very fast, an illusion which quickly disappears.' The jump from second gear to third was massive and without sufficient revs the engine would groan under the strain. With a change back down to second, the motor would scream, but next time enough speed would be built up. With a click into the top cog, the speedometer needle would edge past the 40mph mark.

There were many more lessons that the Bantam novice had to learn. The old myth of slamming on the front brake and going over the handlebars was soon dispelled. Changing gear rapidly down from third to first would be tried only once. Even if the layshaft gears had not stripped their teeth, the most reckless youth would not dare to attempt a repeat performance.

The transmission from the kick-starter by-passed the clutch mechanism so it was possible to start the engine

When happiness was a cheap: ex-GPO Bantam running on L-plates. Note the obligatory dent in the tank courtesy of a damaged bottom steering bracket. (Courtesy Mortons Motorcycle Media)

when any gear was engaged. This was soon picked up by learners and novices and came in very handy when the bike stalled out at road junctions. It saved messing about trying to find neutral.

There was another aspect of motorcycling that was important to the nation's need for people with mechan-

continued overleaf

continued from page 43

ical skills and practical experience. The demise of the Bantam, and of the British motorcycle industry, has indirectly contributed to the subsequent decline of British engineering and other manufacturing bases. The clapped-out and decrepit single-cylinder motorcycle provided the best training ground for scores of fledgling engineers. Anyone who relied on a third-hand BSA Bantam soon became a proficient mechanic! Many young men who struggled at school in maths and science were able to turn their hand to feats of mechanical ingenuity.

My own journey into an engineering trade began with an old Bantam, bought for £7 10s. I cut my engineer's teeth and developed hands-on skills on this rust bucket, which had been dredged up from the canal. My evenings and weekends were spent dissecting and rigging every known dodge to turn it into something dependable and reliable. Parts were smuggled in to the engineering training school, cleaned, fixed, made good and then smuggled out again.

A Bantam could be stripped down to every last component. Even a big-end assembly could be prised apart and re-set on vee blocks during a lunchtime session in the inspection room. I made a new crankpin, had it heat-treated and rebuilt the crank assembly with less than .0015in run-out. I straightened the frame, welded new centre-stand feet (always necessary), and carried out many other repairs.

Today, in the throwaway age, the built-in obsolescence of modern machinery has removed the need for us to call upon our resolve and resource. With recent technological developments, the first vital stepping stones to an education in mechanical engineering have gone.

A Bantam was the cheapest of the cheap. Riding without any insurance was too risky, although many probably did, and the 'Invincible' insurance scheme offered a third-party policy for £2 5s in the 1960s. The annual Ministry of Transport test for vehicle roadworthiness became compulsory from 1960 for vehicles over ten years old, and soon after for those over three years. The idea was to get dilapidated and dangerous cars and motorcycles off the road – quite a few Bantam types probably fell into that group. The MOT never presented any major obstacle to the wise, who knew where to take the vehicle. Most of the old motorcycle shops and second-hand dealers drew up their own rules – the test usually involved some old boy giving the bike a cursory glance and kicking the front tyre, before writing out the certificate.

Andrew Dawson bought his brand-new Sapphire Blue D7 Super in 1965, complete with Avon fairing, Bantam rear carrier and a set of L-plates fixed with black sticky tape. The D7 was a superb learner's bike but was let down by leaky front forks. (Courtesy Andrew Dawson)

Sheila Whittingham pilots her first motorbike in her mother's back garden in Rochdale, Lancashire, 1965. The bike is a 1950 D1 that cost just £2 10 s. Her pillion friend Margaret Taylor cannot contain her excitement. (Courtesy Sheila Whittingham)

There were two road fund licence tax discs available to Bantamites, and both were free. If you lived in the Midlands it was the label off a bottle of Corona lemonade; elsewhere in Britain, a bottle of Guiness could provide something that was about the right size and colour.

After time, the urge to move up from a Bantam became irresistible, but first there was the issue of getting rid of those L-plates.

'Tony A.', who would rather remain anonymous, remembers passing his test on a 150 Major. 'After we did the usual stuff like reading a car number plate from about 30 paces, the examiner told me to start the bike. Would it start? Like hell it would. The engine was still hot so tickling the carb was fatal. There was me kicking it like mad and the examiner pretending to look the other way.

I probably flooded it. Anyway, I managed to do a really good TT-style bump start. The examiner mumbled something about riding around the block so off I went like a little angel, putt-putting slowly along. As soon as I was around the corner, I had the throttle wide open, and my head down on the tank. Every time I came round to the "start-finish" straight, there was the examiner leaning against a wall reading a paper, yawning. For the emergency stop, he stepped out into the road and stuck his hand up. All I had to do was to roll the throttle off; the engine was so clapped out it just stopped dead. Good job, too, because the brakes weren't up to it.'

Tony got his pass, a tiny slip of paper to stick inside his maroon provisional licence. Another pair of L-plates was consigned to the rubbish bin and another maniac was unleashed.

Learning to Ride

The war had given thousands a taste for travel by some mechanized means. Life in the forces provided access to motor vehicles and training in dealing with them, from the thousands who learnt to drive or ride a machine painted in Number 3 Gas-Proof Khaki to the countless others in essential support roles. Many women, for example, distinguished themselves in the fire or auxiliary transport services. The internal combustion engine was no longer a thing to be feared. In the brave new world of the welfare state, nationalized coal, railways and steel, people did not want to go back to their pre-war life. Independent

travel was a now real possibility and the readily available Bantam was a godsend.

For others, however, owning a new Bantam was their first encounter with a motorbike. Apart from learning how to put a bicycle chain back on its sprocket with a stick, or knowing that there is a right way to assemble the leather washer in a bike pump (the standard army test for recruiting Transport Corp from infantry companies), they had little or no other experience. Maintaining a Bantam demanded at least some rudimentary knowledge of simple mechanics. The BSA handbook issued with every machine explained the basics of how to maintain a good spark, adjust the rear chain, change oil and top up the battery (if fitted), and Pitman Publishing soon produced the excellent pocket-sized *Book of the BSA Bantam*, written by technical author H.C. Haycraft (*see* Bibliography). Both the BSA and Pitman book also gave instructions on how to ride a Bantam.

A typical everyday street scene of the 1950s. OPB 210 is a 1950 model. The dual seat has been pinched from a 1000cc V-twin Vincent Rapide. At least someone found a decent use for it! (Courtesy Geoff and Rita Hobbs)

Official BSA catalogue picture of a 1950 D1. Small detail changes from the very early models include the following: exhaust pipe runs over footrest, spring-up centre stand and BSA lettering on primary drive cover. Note the twin fixing screws holding the toolbox lid; later versions had just one. (Courtesy Alistair Cave)

It must have been fun for the novice, out on the road for the first time, to grapple with the controls and weave back and forth as they read: 'To Change Gear (Up). Disengage the clutch and immediately thereafter raise the gear change pedal upwards to its limit, at the same time easing the throttle back. Engage the clutch and reopen the throttle together immediately after changing.' With so many Bantams taking to the roads in the hands of learners, that little Pitman pocket book perched on many a bookshelf, often covered in oily fingerprints.

For BSA, the success of the Bantam cut both ways. Once the L-plates had been removed many former Bantamites traded their bike in for something larger. Badge allegiance played its part in persuading people to buy another BSA. The next step upwards was usually a 250cc C11G or a 350cc B31. Some went all the way and jumped straight on to a 650cc A10 Golden Flash; many were surely caught out by the required down-for-up gearchanges, the opposite to the Bantam. Many others remained faithful to their Bantam, happy to run around for ever on L-plates, and often bestowing affectionate nicknames on their

little friend: some were personal (Gertie, Myrtle or Dotty), while others were more universal (The Phantom Bantam, The Clockwork Cockerel, The Rovin' Rooster or The Flying Fart).

Developments

Some would say that the Bantam was the two-wheel version of the Citroën 2CV, or perhaps the Morris Minor. In historic terms the BSA had more in common with the latter. Both were launched in 1948 and attracted the same amount of regard and trust, as well as the same degree of regret when they both ceased production 23 years later. The eternal 'Moggy Minor' and the Bantam were exported to the same corners of the world, to the far-flung reaches of the British Empire and Commonwealth. In the early years, both dominated their particular market and both went through periodic increases in engine capacity and limited cosmetic changes. The Bantam however, unlike the Morris, which remained a stoical and unabashed family wagon, had sportier aspirations.

As soon as the first rigid-framed models with Wico-Pacy Geni-mag direct lighting trundled on to the streets, BSA realized that the D1 had an appeal for a particularly enthusiastic breed of motorcyclist – the long-distance tourist. Magazines in the 1950s often featured articles written

*Hong Kong 1961.
A plunger-sprung D1
seems to attract interest from
the locals as well as from the
police. (Courtesy Alistair
Cave)*

by motorcyclists who had completed an epic transcontinental tour. The fighting cock was tough enough to survive such a trip, but rear-wheel suspension, offered in late 1949, promised to make the ride even better. The plunger sprung frame allowed for about 3in (7.5cm) of wheel movement. This simple if rudimentary arrangement was a scaled-down version of the kind fitted to larger machines, and consisted of the rear hub carried between sliding yokes and controlled by opposing springs. Provided the yokes were kept well greased, the arrangement worked quite well. Cornering could be exciting, as the plungers could not guarantee equal geometry, but with speeds limited by the average state of roads it hardly caused any anxiety. The rear mudguard fitted to the plunger-type frame retained full valancing from front to back but differed in style from the rigid version. The letter 'S', to denote a springer frame, was added to the normal frame number coding YD1. Some models with a YD2 numbering slipped out, but the attempt to

call the bike the D2 Bantam was short-lived and hastily abandoned.

The standard layout of rigid tail and telescopic front forks for most gave excellent handling and taut cornering, provided the fork bushes were packed full of grease. A basic D1 could drone along for hours at a steady 40mph (65km/h) and on a country road the speed limit was more like 35mph (55km/h). The sprung saddle was comfortable and of ample proportions for a lightweight, but it had such a recoil that any attempt to open up the throttle would result in the rider being tossed into the air like a pancake.

As a further option, a de-luxe Bantam was offered with plunger frame as standard fare along with Lucas coil ignition and DC battery lighting. Well up to the task for supplying reliable night-time lights, the crankshaft carried a contact breaker set and lighting coils with an ignition coil slung underneath the fuel tank. A standard telephone selenium rectifier occupied a space between battery and toolbox. The crankshaft dif-

D1 and D3 models

Engine details

Model series	D1	D3
Year produced	1948–63	1954–57
Capacity	123cc	148cc
Bore × stroke	52 × 58mm	57 × 58mm
Comp ratio	6.5:1	6.4:1
Claimed power	4.5bhp @ 5,000rpm	5.3bhp @ 5,000rpm
Carburation	Amal 361/8	Amal 523/1

Ignition and lighting

D1: Wico-Pacy flywheel magneto. Direct lighting or battery lighting.
D1 De-Luxe (1950-52) only: Lucas generator with coil ignition and battery lighting.

Transmission

		Std	Competition	
Gear ratios	Fourth	N/A	N/A	
	Third	7.0	8.64	7.0
	Second	11.7	14.45	11.7
	First	22.1	27	22.0
Clutch – friction plates		3	3	
Chains – primary				
Size		3/8in × 0.25in	3/8in × 0.25in	
No pitches		50	50	
Rear				
Size		½ × 0.305in		
No pitches		117 (rigid), 123 (plunger)	121 S/A frame	
No sprocket teeth				
Engine		17	17	
Gearbox		15	15	
Clutch Chainwheel		38	38	
Rear Chainwheel		47	58	47

Suspension

	D1	D3
Front	Teles. coil spring, undamped (rubber damped from 1954)	Teles. coil spring, undamped (rubber damped from 1954)
Rear	Rigid, 1948–54. Plunger, 1950–63.	Plunger, 1954–56. S/A, 1956–58.

Capacities

	D1	D3
Fuel tank		
Imp gallons	1¾	1¾
Petroil mixture		
Ratio	20:1	20:1
Gearbox	⅔ pint	⅔ pint

Wheels

Brake size		
Dia	5in	5in
Width	5/8in	5/8in
Rim size		
Front	WM1-19	WM1-19
Rear	WM1-19	WM1-19
Tyre size		
Front	2.75-19	2.75-19
Rear	2.75-19	3.25-19
		2.75-19

Dimensions

Seat height	27½in (687.5mm) (saddle)	29⅛in (737.5mm) (S/A frame)
Wheelbase	50½in (1262.5mm)	51in (1275mm)
Weight (inc 1 gallon of petroil)	170lb (77.25kg) (rigid), 180lb (82kg) (plunger)	217lb (98.6kg) (plunger), 228lb (103.6kg) (S/A frame)

Performance (extracted from published road test data)

Top speed	46mph (74km/h)	52mph (83km/h)
Acceleration	0 to 30mph in 7.8 secs	0 to 30mph in 7.1 secs
Braking distance from 30mph to rest.	32ft	36ft
Fuel consumption	144mpg @ 30mph (1.96ltr/100km @ 48km/h), 112mpg @ 40mph (2.5ltr/100km @ 48km/h)	145mpg @ 30mph (1.95ltr/100km @ 48km/h), 95mpg @ 40mph (2.95ltr/100km @ 48km/h)

fered from the Wico-Pacy versions by having heavier flywheels and a special outer cover, and swapping cranks between the two was impossible.

The Lucas D1 came about because of a shortfall in supply by the Wico-Pacy Corporation, which struggled to keep up with the demand for generators. At one time the manufacture of flywheel magnetos for BSA Bantams accounted for as much as 80 per cent of the company's productivity. Joseph Lucas were requested to respond and eventually orders for 5,000 units were placed. To offset the extra cost, BSA offered the Lucas electrics version at a premium and added the 'De-Luxe' tag. The extra cost for a Lucas Bantam De-Luxe was £6.

From 1953, the Wipac Series 55 Mk 8 generators appeared to replace the more primitive Geni-mag unit. The Series 55 generators were supplied in either AC direct lighting (no engine, no lights) or battery lighting. Theoretically, this allowed for the possibility of swapping generators and fitting a battery and rectifier. Wipac supplied a 'convert-a-kit' to change a direct lighting system to battery lights, although the technology would have been beyond most riders. All models now had a proper electric switch mounted on the headlamp shell though the option of fitting an electric horn to a direct lighting version was not ideal – it sounded like a dying bluebottle trapped in a jam jar. And Bantamites soon realized that, contrary to what they had been told at school, light did not travel in a straight line. It was quite tricky to see ahead by the dull orange glow that spilled out of the headlamp and sploshed all over the road!

Uprating the Bantam

The year 1953 proved to be a special one in many ways, with a new Queen being crowned. The new Elizabethan age brought hopes and expec-

A 1953 125cc D1 plunger (direct lighting) in typical full touring trim. (Courtesy Mick Walker)

Right *Jack Skeers was the BSA agent in Wagga, New South Wales, Australia, in the 1950s. Here he is at the start of the 1954 Redex motorcycle reliability trial on a standard D1 Bantam. (Courtesy Steve Foden, BSAOC)*

Below *BSA advertising in 1954 shows a pair of Bantamites enjoying a clean and healthy outdoor lifestyle. (Courtesy Steve Foden, BSAOC)*

BSA

Bantam
models

OVERSEAS EDITION

The Bantam is a wonderfully successful motor cycle — everybody says so. Now here's an entirely new model — the Bantam Major with a larger capacity engine of 150 c.c., designed to give just that extra power needed by some motorcyclists on some occasions. With Bantam economy and B.S.A. reliability it's going to give a lot of grand service at low cost to thousands of riders.

The 150cc Bantam Major as it appeared in 1954 with a plunger sprung frame and beefed up forks. (Courtesy Steve Foden, BSAOC)

tations for a better and safer world – according to Home Secretary Sir David Maxwell-Fyfe, 'The scourge of Teddy boys was not as widespread as first thought.' Under tough new laws, anyone suspected of driving under the influence of drink had to accompany the Constable back to the station to recite a tongue-twister or walk a white line. Amidst all the celebrations and social changes, the Bantam sold and sold, and then sold some more.

In response to a constant demand for more power, especially from riders who liked to wander the globe with all their worldly possessions bundled on to the back of a Bantam, there was welcome news in October 1953, when BSA announced an uprated model. The 150cc D3 Bantam Major made its debut alongside the 100,000th model D1 at the annual Earls Court show. The press handouts pointed to the logic behind increasing the cylinder bore to 57mm, which would give a slightly under-square unit of 148cc while retaining the original 58mm. Claimed output for the pepped-up Major was 5.2bhp at 5,000rpm, compared with 4.5bhp for

the D1, but the bike still qualified for the lower taxation class. The extra horse was certainly worth having, although the motor had a narrower power band and had to be carefully managed through the gears. Top speed was raised to just over 50mph (80km/h) although 45mph (just over 70km/h) was a more realistic average falling back to 40mph (65km/h) in anything more than a breeze head-on.

A larger 11/16in bore 523/1 Amal carburettor was fitted, still with the spigot fitted bellmouth air strangler. The D3's running gear had heavier front forks, with thicker upper stanchions that had first been committed to the competition D1. Three versions of the D3 were made available, all with sprung frames: a direct-lighting version, a battery-lighting and a Competition. It came in an all-over coat of Pastel Grey and cream tank panels with Bantam Major tank transfers.

The 150 engine from the outset had a new style of cylinder barrel and head with larger finning and increased transfer ports. Inside the crankcases, heavier flywheels and an up-rated big-end bearing, using rollers ¼in (6.25mm) diameter by 3/8in (9.35mm) long, replaced the earlier 7 × 7mm type. The flywheels were recessed at the crankpin eye to take the larger rollers. More significant was a subtle change to improve crankshaft lubrication. The primary drive seal, previously found between the two main bearings, was moved in board up against the flywheel. The left-hand seal was pushed outwards by 0.010in and the crank was extended to suit. This allowed oil drillings to feed lubricant from the primary drive and on to the main bearings. Until then the Bantam engine mainshaft had been entirely dependent upon petroil. To hold it all together two more crankcase fixing screws were added. One was hidden behind the clutch on the right-hand side, leading to many a wrecked right-hand case as a result of the efforts of the average garden-shed engine re-builder!

The humble D1 had also benefited from some of the same attention and the larger fin styling. Gone was the old 'flat Bantam' fishtail silencer. Now all Bantams sported a cigar-shaped silencer with a small conical endpiece with two fins. The new design allowed for a set of baffles to be removed for de-coking – a regular chore for Bantam riders if they were to keep their two-stroke in tune when using the oils available in the 1950s.

The front mudguard arrangement was also revised, with a shallow valanced version, supported from the lower fork stanchions. A little later, the headlamp received a cowl design mounting bracket. Another detail change that was applied on the introduction of the D3 – and should have been introduced much earlier – was swapping the fuel filler cap over from the left to the right-hand side of the fuel tank. This was to prevent neat mixing oil being poured straight down the fuel tap and clogging up the carburettor. The gear position indicator, another relic inherited from the DKW RT125, which occupied a spot near the gearbox sprocket, also disappeared.

The following year all-black options for the D1 and D3 were offered. As chromium supply

A restored 1957 150cc D3 Bantam Major in Pastel Grey. (Owen Wright)

Blissful and carefree days, when D1 Bantam pillion riders wore cotton summer dresses and stiletto heels. The scene is Shakespeare's birthplace in Stratford upon Avon. The scooter across the road is the very rare 1955 BSA 250cc 'Beesa', which did not go into production. (Courtesy Steve Foden, BSAOC)

restrictions were lifted, due to the Korean War, bright plated wheel rims were adopted as standard across the entire range of BSAs from 1954. The Bantam even received a pair of dashing chrome-plated strips covering the tank ribs.

At this time, BSA had re-launched its very popular 250cc OHV and SV single-cylinder 'C' models with alternator electrics. The sidevalve C10 had been re-engineered to use what was basically a plunger D1 Bantam frame. Not quite the four-stroke Bantam that some may have hoped for, the last of the old sidevalvers, now called the C10L, was an ugly hybrid finished in Mist Green with contrasting dark green tank panelling.

The changes made to both the 125 and 150cc engines in 1955 was to cause some irritation to the home mechanic. The spacing of the cylinder barrel studs was increased to accommodate a larger-diameter barrel spigot. In compensation, and to complicate the matter even further, a spacing collar was fitted between the left-hand flywheel and main bearing. The new crankcase castings meant that neither the cylinder barrels nor crankcases were interchangeable between pre- and post-1955 models.

The range of colours increased with the addition of maroon; like the black paint finish, however, it was commonly found on the D3 but rarely on the D1. Mist Green remained the favourite colour for the latter. In 1956, the Bantam brood was also rationalized, with the D1 and D3 Competition models being phased out, along with the old rigid-frame D1. The plunger-frame '150' was abandoned too, bringing to an end the best of a lusty engine in a lightweight frame.

The D3 Bantam Major now came with a modern swing-arm chassis using Girling telescopic shock absorbers and the trailing arm supported with rubber bushings. Such sophistication gave excellent road-hugging and a more stable support for a dual seat, even the all-up weight had gone up to 225lb.

The rear section was a very heavy-duty tube and brazed lug affair with triangulated side panels, housing a toolbox and battery (if fitted) and following a style and format established by the larger OHV BSAs. The swing-arm D3 came with a new-type long tapered silencer, which improved engine breathing, and removable baffles. Its contribution to better performance was such that even D1 owners fitted one as best they could.

A D3 Major in swing-arm frame was tested by *The Motorcycle* in July 1956. 'Ample power for touring, fuel economy and docility in traffic among the attributes of a striking two-stroke lightweight' ran the headline. The report loved its handling and brakes but disliked that irritating little horn button built in-situ with the front brake lever. The exhaust was also described – in 1950s language – as 'disconcerting'.

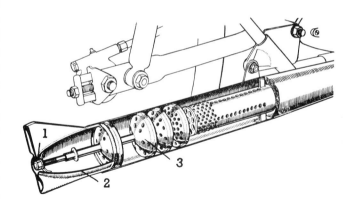

Above *An efficient silencer with easily detachable baffles was introduced with the 1956 swing-arm 150cc D3 Bantam Major.*

Below *A swing-arm 150cc D3 Bantam Major finished in optional maroon. (Owen Wright)*

Political Change at Home and Abroad

Just as Britain was making a steady recovery, with continued growth in manufacturing, along came the Suez crisis. Sir Anthony Eden had succeeded Sir Winston Churchill at Number 10 in 1955 and in the following year he sent the British fleet out to seize the Suez Canal and topple Egyptian President Colonel Nasser. Although the escapade was a military success, the political fiasco that ensued, and the severe disruption to oil supplies to the refineries, showed that Britain could no longer police the world with a gunboat. How ironic that Eden (later Lord Avon) was the bigwig who ceremoniously cut the ribbon that celebrated the 100,000th fuel-miserly Bantam.

The turmoil in world politics extended to the BSA industrial empire, as the company's head-line-grabbing ruling dynasty was ousted. In November 1957, company Chairman Sir Bernard Docker and his wife Lady Norah were ejected in a very public and untidy boardroom war. With allegations of illicit money dealings already filed against Docker, the couple were voted off the board once and for all time by a faction led by Jack Young Sangster. 'Mr Jack', as the papers liked to call him, had rescued the Ariel and Triumph motorcycle companies in the 1930s. Although these two famous names retained their own brand identity and acted as autonomous companies, they had been absorbed into the BSA empire since the early 1950s. As the 1960s approached, some cross-pollination of engineering between BSA, Triumph and Ariel began to be evident.

The fortunes of J.Y. Sangster were to some extent tied up with the irascible genius of Edward

This beautifully restored D1 Competition model is now something of a rarity. Note the upswept exhaust, adjustable footrests and a folding kick-start. (Dennis Bates)

Turner, who had presented Sangster and his companies with some exceptional ideas, including the 1000cc OHC Ariel Square-Four (an audacious 4-cylinder design on which the cylinders were arranged in the form of a square) and the sleek and silky 500cc Triumph Speed twin of 1936.

Overhauling the BSA Range

The changes high up within BSA were to have repercussions all the way down to the humble BSA Bantam. With the appointment of Edward Turner as head of BSA-Triumph Automotive, it would only be a matter of time before the whole BSA range had a complete and overdue facelift.

In the late 1950s the magic of the 125cc D1 had begun to fade and the 150cc D3 gave way to a new breed of 175cc Bantam Super. There was a half-hearted attempt to re-name the D1 as the Bantam Minor, but it never quite caught on. More colour options were made available, including Ruby Red, and the 125cc engine shared the benefits of Bantam Super development, with all models having a further improved big-end bearing.

The D3 had been put out as a longer-legged touring version of the basic D1, but the extra metal of a swing-arm frame had sapped some of its strength. The eventual capacity increase to 175cc was an active response by BSA to satisfy the never-ending demand for more power.

The scooter mania of the late 1950s and early 1960s did affect the market, but contemporary lightweight motorcycles from other manufactures had seldom threatened the Bantam's domination. The Bantam had so far shrugged off any challenges. The Velocette LE 'Noddy bike' flat-twin sidevalve was too complex, too unorthodox and too expensive. Eventual Bantam buyers might have considered the Triumph Terrier, a 150cc OHV single that was superbly styled in the best Triumph tradition and sold well after it appeared in 1952. The later 200cc Tiger Cub was another strong favourite in the lightweight class. It had a mellow exhaust note and a strong punchy engine that must have made many Bantam owners envious. (At the same time, Tiger Cub riders

worried about the gear whine, tappet rattle and piston slap, and probably wished they had a Bantam!) The competitors were usually powered by a Villiers 9E, housed in a James, Cotton, Greeves or DMW. With a strong, capable motor built in the finest Black Country tradition, the infernal 1950s two-stroke motorcycles supplied by Associated Motorcycles Ltd, and other independents, gave good performance but they could never match the price and easy availability of the Bantam, which continued to pour out from BSA's huge production facilities.

Throughout the 1950s, BSA produced some completely new two-stroke machines but each one failed to live up to expectations. A 35cc 'Winged Wheel' clip-on cyclemotor was technically good but arrived too late. Of more significance, a 98cc sleeved-down Bantam engine, with two-speed gear, low-slung frame, leading link forks and 15in wheels, was tried but dropped. The wheels and forks eventually featured in the 1956 70cc Dandy Scooterette, an imaginative but over-sophisticated device that had a penchant for seizing its engine. Despite its failure, it was a precursor to the step-thru mopeds that came later from the Far East in massive numbers. However hard it tried, it seemed that BSA would never build another two-stroke as successful as the Bantam.

The End of the Little Green Machine

The truth about the origins of the Bantam remained a secret until the early 1960s. Until then, no one had dared to mention the link with wartime German machines, and the story had not come out, not even in any of the road tests, handouts, tuning tips or weekly publications. A search through the official literature of the early 1950s reveals no mention of the way in which BSA managed to pull a successful two-stroke out of the hat. In his history of BSA, *The Giants of Small Heath*, a book dealing with the rise and fall of BSA as a company, author Barry Ryerson claims that the first mention of the Bantam's DKW origins appeared in an issue of the BSA Owners Club journal *The Star*. Readers responded by shrugging their shoulders. They were more concerned with reports about the Japanese, who were studying and copying British cars and motorcycles in every detail, right down to manufactured imperfections such as machining marks.

The D1 struggled on, with only fresh orders for GPO telegram delivery machines propping it up. In its last year, annual factory production figures for 1963–64 recorded 709 model D1s; of these, 600 went to the GPO, and just 80 battery and 29 direct lighting versions were destined for private use. By then the D7 Bantam Super (and its derivatives) had been established, with just over 3,700 built and shipped. As telegram services receded, the GPO opted for the D7 to fulfil its needs for postal delivery work, and the life of the little green motorcycle came to an end. The future for the much-loved and easy-selling Bantam was still bright but it would find the going a lot harder.

Opposite *'Telegram, Sir!' One of the first BSA D1 Bantam GPO telegram delivery bikes at your service. JXY 899 was issued in 1950 and requisitioned to Leicester, Charles Street. (Courtesy John Hollins, Leicester Mercury)*

The Little Red Rooster (GPO Bantams)

Long before e-mail and the Internet, the fastest and most efficient way to send a written message was by electric telegram, although it was fairly expensive for the average household. The transmitting and receiving stations were run and maintained by the General Post Office but treated as an extension of the telephone network. Once a message had been printed out on to a card, an impetuous young lad would race across town on a little red motorcycle and deliver it to the recipient.

Since the late 1920s a 250cc BSA of one type or another gradually became the preferred GPO motorcycle for telegram deliveries. Countless other types were tried and discarded in an effort to find a low-cost reliable bike. In the immediate post-war years, the GPO began to dabble with low-powered 98cc Autocycles but then along came the BSA Bantam.

The GPO took its first delivery of fifty D1 Bantams in December 1948 for telegram deliveries. It immediately became the standard-issue machine, complete with legshields, parcel racks and canvas pannier bags. The first batch were supplied in Mist Green, before the adoption of the all-red livery, with gold GPO decals running down each legshield, a 'T'-prefixed serial number and the cipher of King George VI on the tank. As the GPO was a government body, centralized buying and control procedures meant that every Bantam carried a London registration number. A 'Defence of the Realm Certificate' exempted them from carrying a licence disc, and this system that lasted until 1969 when the organization was split into separate telephone and postal services.

Telegram delivery boys had to be 16, smart and courteous, and were required to ride with all due care and attention, in accordance with the Highway Code. However, as one ex-GPO worker, who was stationed in the main Leicester sorting office, recalls, 'I used to watch the little buggers racing out of the main sorting office. There was a roundabout near the main entrance, and they had this little game to see who could make the most sparks by grounding the footrests!'

The machines entrusted to these young men in dark blue uniforms were supposed to be restricted to 30mph but, as the lads carried out their own maintenance, there was always ways and means of overcoming the GPO-specified governing devices. Some would use a washer surreptitiously shoved into the inlet port, others an extra-long throttle slide fitted into the carburettor.

In addition to the speed-restricting devices, GPO Bantams were covered by very stringent specifications, relating to all sorts of elements, from the gauge thickness of the wheel spokes to the position of the toolbox. One typical quirk was the fitting of a 'D'-style speedo reading up to 70mph (on a 30mph-restricted machine), instead of the normal D1 type with a 55mph face. On completion of a batch of machines, members of the GPO inspectorate would visit BSA and laboriously measure and check every feature on every machine. One by one each bike was wheeled out and checked to see if it could achieve its minimum turning circle. They even measured the length of the canvas pannier bag straps!

The life of a GPO Bantam was expected to be between five and seven years, depending upon the location. One machine, MLH 199 (T2809), was eventually

continued on page 60

continued from page 58

replaced after eleven years in service. If anything more serious than normal maintenance was needed the bike could be shipped off to a central repair depot. One of the main locations was at Yeading near Hayes in Middlesex, where mechanics carried out overhauls on all types of GPO vehicles. Bantams went in for a re-fit every 15,000

miles (25,000km) after which they would return to duty totally rejuvenated and gleaming in a fresh coat of Post Office Red.

As telephone use began to become more widespread during the early 1960s, the need for a telegram delivery service declined. GPO records show that the last batch of 125cc D1s were received in September 1965, a couple of years after BSA officially discontinued production. The change to the 175cc D7 and the later four-speed D10 was inevitable and the final deliveries during 1969–71 consisted of 500 B175s (fitted with D7 barrels). Some of

A line-up of 1966 GPO D7 models occupy the paving outside the BSA factory in Armoury Road, Small Heath. (Courtesy Steve Foden, BSAOC)

continued on page 62

Above *The last of the GPO Bantams. Near-side view of a B175 destined for postal duty with special carrier, first aid kit, and GRP legshields. (Courtesy John Lawrence)*

Right *Close-up detail of GPO-issue B175. Note D1-style tubular silencer, D7 head and barrel and restricted Amal carburettor. (Courtesy John Lawrence)*

continued from page 60

these machines were mothballed and never saw service until 1974.

The total number of Bantams sold to the GPO numbered 6,574, which included 775 early rigid-frame D1s, 4,611-plunger frame D1s. The last pair of Bantams, then operating in Sunderland, were pensioned off on 1 October 1982 having completed ten years of service. One of these machines has survived and has been preserved for posterity.

There was little public demand for pensioned-off ex-GPO Bantams, most of which had been run ragged by a succession of young tearaways. Paul Marlow remembers spotting a public notice in Kettering Post Office, mentioning the disposal of former GPO 125cc BSA motorcycles; sealed bids were to be submitted forthwith. He scrawled a note offering a cheeky 30 shillings and handed it in at the counter when his turn came. A few days later, a letter arrived from the area Post Office manager: 'Thank you for your offer. When are you coming to collect it?'

Today, a genuine ex-GPO Bantam carries a lot more kudos. Probably the most famous Bantam that once carried the Post Office livery is Project 9, a 1955 D1 that came into the possession of John B. Storey in 1965. Project 9, registration RLB 459, has completed 300,000 miles (nearly 500,000km) and is still going strong. It has

A large batch of D1 Bantams were supplied to the South African Postal Service in 1950. (Courtesy Alistair Cave)

been ridden to 23 countries, including Poland, Hungary, the former Yugoslavia and Eastern Germany when it was the DDR. It was once ridden around the complete circuit of London's orbital motorway, the M25, and to this day could be claim to be the oldest and smallest vehicle to do the trip. John Storey is the first to admit that his bike is far removed from the polished bikes that show up at *concours d'elegance* events as you can get. Project 9 stands as testament to the sheer durability of the Bantam. As Storey points out in one of his frequent articles in *The Independent*, the magazine of the British Two-Stroke Club, a Japanese bike would not run with the same faults.

There is now a resurgence of interest for ex-Post Office vehicles, with Chris Hogan and the Post Office Vehicle Club ensuring that the GPO Bantam will live on. Other champions of the all-red Bantams are John and Kate Lawrence, who have collected a number of wrecks and restored them to their former glory. The Lawrence collection, based in Barrow-in-Furness, Cumbria, comprises an impressive line-up of true-to-life GPO Bantams (including one previously owned and ridden by me – a 1964 D1, registration ALC 23B, which was once coated in blue household emulsion and held together with sticky tape. Now it is proudly blushing red again.)

Above *One of the last batches of GPO D1 Bantams is prepared ready for despatch, May 1962. (Courtesy Alistair Cave)*

Right *The evergreen Project 9 in 1983. Owned by John Storey, RLB 459 is a 1955 ex-GPO D1 that has covered 300,000 known miles (over 480,000km) and is still going strong. (Owen Wright)*

Some GPO Bantams live for ever! This 1964 ex-GPO D1 freshly restored by John Lawrence belongs to an extensive collection. (Owen Wright)

GPO Register: Summary of GPO BSA Bantam Purchases

(Reproduced by kind permission of the Post Office Vehicle Club: © Post Office Vehicle Club 2001)

Serial number	Registration	Frame Number	Engine Number	Registration Date
D1 rigids				
T1787–T1836	JYY 934–983	YD1 7051–7100		December 1948
T1837–T1886	KGO 1–50	YD1 10001–10050	YD1 5631–5680	March–April 1949
T1889–T1988	JXY 180–279	YD1 122001–122100		December 1949
T1989–T2088	JXY 830–929	YD1 122101–122200		January 1950
T2186–T2659	KYT 526–999	YD1 122201–122674		December 1950 to April 1951
T2660	LUU 564	YD1 122675		April 1951
D1 plunger				
T2664–T3002	MLH 54–392	YD1S 75000–75338	YD 122811–123149	March 1952
T3003–T3267	MYF 493–757	YD1S 83000–83264	YD 123150–123414	October 1952
D1 plunger with later style of front mudguard				
T3268–T3367	NGJ 502–601	BD2S 10001–10100	BD2 5001–5100	September 1953
T3368–T3467	NGJ 602–701	BD2S 10101–10200	BDB 5101–5200	October 1953
T3468–T3627	PGO 668–827	BD2S 40001–40160	BDB 5201–5360	January 1955
T3628–T3927	RLB 160–459	BD2S 55001–55300	DDB 5362–5661	September–October 1955
T3928–T4146	RXT 661–879	BD2S 60000–60218	DDB 5662–5880	January–April 1956
T4147–T4526	SLO 583–962	BD2S 60219–60598	DDB 5881–6260	June/July 1956
T4527–T4542	TGC 274–289	BD2S 61492–61507	DDB 6271–6286	October 1956
T4543–T4649	TGC 893–999	BD2S 63000–63106	DDB 7001–7107	September 1957
T4650–T4692	TUV 1– 43	BD2S 63107–63149	DDB 7108–7150	September 1957
T4693–T4742	TUV 912–961	BD2S 66000–66049	DDB 8301–8350	March 1958
T4743–T4792	UXH 921–970	BD2S 66050–66099	DDB 10101–10150	March 1958
T4793–T4942	UXV 100–249	BD2S 66100–66249	DDB 10151–10300	March and June 1958
T4943–T5002	UXV 250–309	BD2S 66601–66660	DDB 10311–10370	June 1958
T5003–T5263	WLA 327–587	BD2S 69000–69260	DDB 11401–11661	March 1959
T5264–T5529	YLH 101–366	BD2S 72001–72266	DDB 13251–13516	April 1960
T5530–T5904	1–375 BXE	BD2S 75000–75374	DDB 15201–15575	March 1961
T5911–T5999	682–770 DLF	BD2S 78001–78089	DDB 17001–17089	May 1962
T14000–T14228	771–999 DLF	BD2S 78090–78318	DDB 17090–17318	May–July 1962
T14229–T14255	1– 27 DXV	BD2S 78319–78345	DDB 17319–17345	July 1962
T14284–T14317	966–999 FXY	BD2S 81000–81033	DDB 18514–18547	October 1963
T14318–T14583	715–980 FYM	BD2S 81034–81299	DDB 18548–18813	October–December 1963
T14584–T14933	ALC 1–350B	BD2S 81301–81650	DDB 18814–19163	June/July 1964
T14934–T15090	GLE 843–999C	BD2S 82001–82157	DDB 19201–19357	September 1965
T15091–T15308	GLU 1–218C	BD2S 82158–82375	DDB 19358–19575	September 1965
D7				
T15327–T15526	KVB 757–956D	HD7 101–300	HD7 101–300	December 1966
D10				
T15578–T15742	SYM 494–658F	BD10 101–265	BD10 101–265	December 1967
T15743–T15842	SLU 840–939F	BD10 266–365	BD10 266–365	July 1968
T15844–T15963	locally registered	JCO 3001–3120	3001–3120	1969/1970
B175				
T282860–T282959	locally registered	JCO 5001–5100	ADO 5001–5100	1970
T283085–T283484	locally registered	JCO 7101–7500	07101–07500 (prefix XD, AE or BE)	1970–1973

3 Middle-Aged Spread (The D5–D7 Models)

The late 1950s saw a boom in consumer spending, especially in the areas of white goods and private motor transport. 'Most of our people have never had it so good,' claimed British Prime Minister Harold Macmillan, speaking in Bradford in July 1957. The feelgood factor of the growing economy was so strong, it swept 'Super Mac' back into Downing Street in autumn 1959. The Bantam was in the thick of the frenzied sales of motorcycles and scooters. During the late 1950s, every domestic appliance seemed to have a chromium-plated 'Super' strip stuck on it somewhere. It was a favourite selling trick throughout British industry, and the announcement of a 'Super' Bantam was almost inevitable. The first 175cc BSA Bantam D5 'Super' was launched in autumn 1957.

Developing the D5 Super

Bantam engine development had been transferred from Redditch to Small Heath in 1956. At first, an attempt to build a 197cc version around a 57 × 72mm configuration had to be aborted. The prototype had the performance but vibrated badly due to very heavy flywheels, and the extra torque ripped out the chain adjusters. In the end the engineers resorted to the old trick of increasing the bore size, thus avoiding a complete re-design of the engine. Keeping to the 58mm stroke the new engine cylinder was carved out to 61.5mm, giving an over-square swept volume of 174cc. The compression ratio also leapt up to 7.4:1.

During the last months of 1957, with the 125cc D1 still in production and the 150cc D3 yet to be phased out, the Bantam was actually produced in all three engine sizes. Owner's handbooks and parts manuals referred to the latest 175cc version as the 'D5 Major', although a 'Bantam Super' badge was varnished on to the tank as the last consignment of D3 150 Majors left the works. The new bike, still very much in the tried and trusted Bantam mould, promised more heart and longer legs for faster travel over greater distances. The D5 Super was often shown in full touring trim, with a Motor Plastic Company detachable windscreen and legshields. These, and the useful add-on of a rear carrier, were all available as BSA-supplied extras. The MPC windscreen, made by a BSA subsidiary, had established itself as an effective weather barrier and was catalogued as the 'Bantam Major Screen', price £2 13 s.

As a basic follow-up on the old 150 swing-arm Major, the D5 Super used much of the existing frame and cycle parts, but a fatter, rounder 2-gallon fuel tank and smaller 18in wheels gave it a more balanced stance. There was a penchant for triangular toolboxes and side panels, shared by just about every company in the trade, and the D5 received one the size of a dinner plate, adding to the 'big-bike' image. Rated at 7.5bhp, the first 175 engine could be pulled away in top gear from 15mph (25km/h) and run all the way up to a top speed of 60mph (95km/h) on the flat; it cruised easily at 55mph (90km/h) all day with no bother and still returned 100mpg (2.8ltr/100km). Most owners probably claimed even better results, refusing to listen to hard scientific evidence that a standard Smiths 'D'-shaped, non-o-jewels speedometer always flattered by 10 per cent.

The first 175cc Bantam was at first called a D5 'Major'. The awkward-looking toolbox is from a D3 model, which suggests that this BSA publicity picture depicts the production bike in the autumn of 1957. (Courtesy Steve Foden, BSAOC)

The new 175 brought in an improved big-end bearing using rollers of 4mm diameter and 8mm long, held in duralumin half-cages, and a series of radial drillings in the big-end eye to improve oil flow. It was a substantial improvement on the earlier crowded roller types; BSA's engineers had obviously been studying bearing design and practice found on the latest continental machinery.

The enlarged cylinder took a flange-mounted type 375 7/8in (21mm) choke Amal monobloc carburettor. Anyone thinking about instantly uprating a D1 with a D5 barrel and head would come to grief. The spacing of the cylinder fixing studs had been further opened out to 60mm. A new type of bonded-on Neolangite-faced friction plate was introduced to all Bantams at this time in place of the old cork insert type. That put a stop to owners making new inserts by cutting up old wine bottle corks!

There was some extra stopping power too, with both front and rear 5in diameter brake shoes increased in width to 7/8in (21mm). The smaller wheels meant a change in overall gearing with the gearbox sprocket gaining an extra tooth, going up to 16T, and the rear wheel sprocket losing one, going down to 46T. This welcome change produced a bike that retained everything that was good about the Bantam – ample low speed and torque that kept going through the whole range and a motor that could take any amount of abuse. With a three-speed gearbox and the evergreen Wico-Pacy flywheel magneto, this

Left *The 175cc D5 Bantam Super used much of the previous 150cc frame and cycle parts. Otherwise, the tank and toolbox were restyled and the wheels were 18in diameter. The brakes were also increased in size to match the additional power. (Courtesy Steve Foden, BSAOC)*

Below *When Tom Doubtfire bought this 1958 175cc D5 Super it had been owned by the former driver of a steam locomotive based in Stoke on Trent. Some parts of it had been treated to a liberal coating of heavy-duty British Railways black enamel! (Owen Wright)*

was a machine that offered amazing value and sound engineering.

The D5 Super came in either all-over Bayard Crimson (maroon) or black with broad and expansive ivory tank panels, with a Bantam Super motif and a single chrome-plated strip running down the centre.

Of the two versions of the D5 Super, direct or battery lighting, the latter was priced at £127 4s 11d, including purchase tax. David Brindley bought his maroon and ivory Bantam D5 Super in May 1958. He was 17 and was starting to earn £20 per month. His new mode of transport was financed by a hire purchase deal, at £4 12s and 6d a month. With no previous experience of motorcycling he set about carefully running in his Bantam using Filtrate graphite two-stroke oil.

It fouled the engine up, and this could only be cleared by removing the crankcase drain plug and revving it to blazes. By the end of the year, Brindley had passed his test and had covered 10,000 miles (16,000km). The Bantam ate its way through countless spark plugs and wore out a pair of fork bushes. With 15,126 miles (24,202km) on the clock, one of the gudgeon pin circlips made a hasty exit through the piston, followed by a series of punctures and broken cables and a couple of worn-out chains. Brindley's ownership of 698 CKP came to an end in December 1959, after 22,840 miles (36,545km), when its main bearings failed. Compton and Ecclestones of Bexleyheath obliged with a brand-new Ariel Leader 250cc two-stroke twin.

Fowl Pest

The life of a Bantam depended upon the key factors of maintenance, and the riding technique and mechanical aptitude of the owner. Some machines received the proper scheduled servicing, others were worked on with a lump hammer and a blunt screwdriver. Some were stored in a dry garage, others slung against the coalhouse. Some were freely revved with correct use of the gears, others were regularly flogged up hills in top gear. It made all the difference.

The methods of mass production used by the motor industry were less than ideal. Parts were knocked out and stockpiled in large batches. Manufacturing tolerances were wide and quality control depended upon manual inspection and statistics that fell far short of guaranteeing zero defects. Seemingly, no two machines were identical, and the Bantam certainly had a number of in-built deficiencies and design faults.

The concentric kick-start and gear-change shafts proved to be the most prominent mechanical weakness, causing owners more torment than anything else. The levers were located on serrated shafts and secured with a pinch bolt. Constant vibration invariably caused the bolt to loosen, the serrations stripped, leaving either lever incapable of transmitting effort through its mating shaft. The serrations on the DKW RT125-based prototype were coarse and certainly much stronger. The finer machined type that was put into production was a 1947 commercial compromise to use existing tooling from the Sunbeam S7. Owners turned to a vast array of solutions, from the futile use of nails and matchsticks, to epoxy resin and black sticky tape rammed between the two divorced components. More skilled owners could drill through the shaft and lever to fit a cross-pin, and the most drastic remedial ploy was to braze the lever directly to the shaft. The best way of dealing with the problem, at least to get you home, was to bind some tape or emery cloth around the damaged serrations before carefully locating the lever.

The gear change return spring could last either five minutes or five decades. If it broke, gear changing was still possible but very awkward as the lever had to be gently lifted and prodded with a sensitive toe. Replacement meant splitting the engine apart, so it was recommended at any suitable opportunity – a shilling and ninepence for a genuine BSA replacement was money well spent.

The kick-starter return spring rarely gave out and did a smart job. Trouble began when the engine was taken apart and the the spring had to be re-wound to the correct tension. Many a Bantam kick-start lever bounced up and down or had to be supplemented with bungee straps or large rubber bands cut from bicycle inner tubes.

continued overleaf

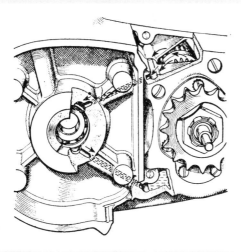

Above *A new Bantam such as this 1965 D7 De-Luxe would provide many thousands of miles of reliable service, but after a few years, the crankshaft seals would begin to wear and the forks to leak oil, and the kick-start and gear-lever shafts would frequently work loose. It would all end with a no-go engine, appalling brakes, a fake leopard-skin seat cover and that once-flamboyant red finish covered by a thick layer of Woolworth's brushing enamel. (Courtesy Alistair Cave)*

Left *During 1954 positive lubrication for the left-hand main bearing was introduced. Drillings in the crankcase allowed an oil feed from the gearbox to prolong the life expectancy of the main shaft bearings. Previously, the bearings relied purely on oil deposits from petroil lubrication.*

continued from page 69

On the early D1 models, over-gearing and a common aversion to revving the motor caused condensation within the crankcases. The main crankshaft bearings would often rust before they wore out. This was later overcome when the engine main bearings received lubricant from the gearbox and primary drive. On all models, good crankcase compression was vital; damaged or worn crank seals were one of the main reasons for dismal performance.

The aluminium castings carried Whitworth threads, a coarse 55-degree form that was very strong, and stripped threads in sand-cast crankcases were rare. Later die-cast components were more brittle. Some parts were threaded with British Standard Fine (or BSF), finer form with more threads per linear inch, giving a profile that was smaller and less strong but gave better locking. The cylinder head studs were screwed into the crankcases with BSW but fitted with BSF nuts for securing the cylinder head. Stripped cylinder head nuts and studs were fairly common thanks to over-zealous use of the

The 1969–71 B175 engine was one of the best and most reliable Bantam units.
The introduction of Unified thread forms was a belated move to keep in step with
the automotive industry even though a general move towards metric threads was in
progress. The circular air filter fixed to the Amal concentric carburettor was a feature
found on the 1966–67 D10 models. (Owen Wright)

continued from page 70

spanner, as cold fingers struggled to contrive cross-threading of the offending nut. The matter was easily rectified with a new stud and nut, although fitting an extra washer to give the nut a thread to bite on was a favourite bodge. Elsewhere, fine 26 teeth per inch 60-degree called CEI, later British Standard Cycle, would be found particularly on the frame and cycle parts. To complicate matters further, the 1969 B175 models introduced Unified thread forms. A replacement rear swing-arm suspension pin would look identical to a D14/4 type except that the threaded holes for the locating bolts were UNF not BSF.

Cheese-head screws with plain slots, used on the engine unit, did not like repeated undoing and tightening. Chewed or broken screw heads are a certainty on a second-hand Bantam. Crosshead screws came in with the D7 and were a vast improvement.

The clutch was generally a trouble-free unit. On early models, the friction plates carried cork inserts. These could break up, spraying tiny cork granules around the internals, clogging up bearing oilways. Later models were fitted with Neolangite material bonded to the plate. Any Bantam with more than 40,000 miles on the clock is now likely to have the later-type friction plates in place. The clutch assembly was bound together with six compression springs and then locked into the main clutch drum

Regular use of the grease gun was essential if the plunger rear suspension units fitted to D1 and early D3 models were to survive and operate. (Owen Wright)

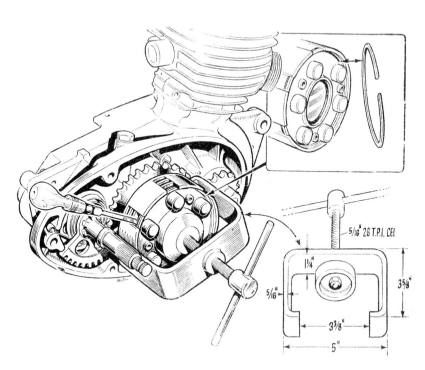

Every home should have one: the recommended clutch spring compressor tool.
Attempting to dismantle the clutch without this tool could result in serious injury.

with a large rectangular-section circlip. A clutch spring compressor tool tool was vital, to hold the assembly together, to enable the circlip to be prised out of its groove. The clutch could be released without this special tool, but the six springs would shoot out like bullets. Even if the springs were still intact, the task of undoing was far easier than putting them back together again, trying to keep six springs compressed with one hand and the circlip pushed into its groove.

Oil leaks were surprisingly few, although a small amount of half-burnt oil would creep out from the exhaust port and the underside of the engine unit would always feature a drip. Gearbox oil would weep from the primary cover and from the gearbox sprocket seal housing. If leaks from the casings were persistent it usually signalled the worst sin of the inept home mechanic: using a screwdriver to prise the crankcase halves apart, leaving a channel for oil to run through. Oozing globules of gasket cement indicate this nasty affliction; extreme cases have to be repaired with the skilled use of Lumiweld.

Equally unacceptable was the use of a chisel or screwdriver to dislodge the gearbox filler and drain plugs, and then to tighten them again. The fibre washers would be well and truly chewed and then asked to do another tour of duty.

A misfire would often be attributed to something in the carburettor, because of the complications of the electrical apparatus, and therefore left alone. However, the carb would come to pieces easily. In certain instances, the carb may well have been at fault. It did not like specks of grit, dirt, rust and dismembered insects, which somehow managed to squeeze past the fuel tap or air filter. The main and pilot jet carrier was easy to remove, blow out and re-fit. The float chamber would collect fine particle debris after a time and some would eventually block the gallery leading into the jet block. The later alloy throttle slides wore faster than the older brass versions. Persistent carburettor troubles were often traced to worn-out float

continued overleaf

continued from page 73

needles, the ill-advised use of a piece of steel wire to clear a blocked jet or a distorted mounting flange on the later monobloc or concentric fittings.

On the move the Bantam was resilient and hardy, but susceptible to certain types of abuse. Prolonged 'pinking' of the engine, due to any combination of bad timing, worn points or a decrepit spark plug, would eventually lead to disaster, with a hole burnt straight through the piston crown. A sudden change from top gear down into first would strip the teeth from the gearbox layshaft. Jumping out of gear was down to a worn selector camplate, and a whirling sound that continued after the engine had been stopped was due either to noisy layshaft bearings or to the flywheel compression plates being loosened from their resting place. On D14/4 models a set of rivets holding the plates to the flywheel caused many a mechanical apocalypse. The D10 series also had the rep-

Anyone looking for a potential restoration project should expect to find all kinds of anomalies and non-standard fittings. The rounded bolt heads and dreaded screwdriver marks under the crankcases are inevitable, however. This 175cc D7 Super advertised for sale (offers invited) at an autojumble has a high-torque cylinder head. (Owen Wright)

utation of being the least reliable of the brood on account of the lofty steps in power output without the corresponding increases in crankshaft diameter.

Any problems were usually electrical. No lights, no spark, coughing, spitting, banging or a drastic loss of power could usually be traced to a faulty condenser, bad wiring or some other electrical problem. The source would more often than not lie in that mysterious contraption that lurked behind a circular cover – the dreaded Wico-Pacy flywheel magneto. For more on the physics of these electro-magnetic devices, see Chapter 6.

The innards of a Wico-Pacy Series 55 Mk 8 flywheel generator on a battery-lighting version. Electronic ignition units are now readily available to liven up a tired old ignition generator. (Owen Wright)

Fit
LODGE
SPARK PLUGS
and feel the difference!

All Bantamites used to carry a bag of pink-bodied Lodge spark plugs.

D5 and D7 models

Engine details

Model series	D5	D7
Year produced	1958	1959–66
Capacity	174cc	174cc
Bore × stroke	61.5 × 58mm	61.5 × 58mm
Comp ratio	7.4:1	7.4:1
Claimed power	7.4bhp @ 4,750rpm	7.4bhp @ 4,750rpm
Carburation	Amal 375 Monobloc	Amal 375 Monobloc

Ignition and lighting

D5: Wico-Pacy flywheel magneto. Direct lighting or battery lighting.
D7: Wico-Pacy flywheel magneto. Direct lighting or battery lighting. Some models supplied with coil ignition.

Transmission

		D5	D7
Gear ratios	Fourth	N/A	N/A
	Third	6.5	6.58
	Second	10.74	11.10
	First	20.2	20.65
Clutch – friction plates		3	3
Chains – primary			
Size		3/8in × 0.25in	3/8in × 0.25in
No pitches		50	50
Rear			
Size		½in × 0.335in	½in × 0.335in
No pitches		121	121
No sprocket teeth			
Engine		17	17
Gearbox		15	15
Clutch Chainwheel		38	38
Rear Chainwheel		46	46

Suspension

	D5	D7
Front	Teles. coil spring, rubber damped	Teles. coil spring, hydraulically damped
Rear	Swing-arm. Girling spring-hyd units	Swing-arm. Girling spring-hyd units

Capacities

	D5	D7
Fuel tank		
Imp gallons	2	1 7/8 (De-Luxe)
Petroil mixture		
Ratio	20:1	20:1
Gearbox	¾ pint	¾ pint

Wheels

	D5	D7
Brake size		
Dia	5in	5½in
Width	7/8in	1in
Rim size		
Front	WM1-18	WM1-18
Rear	WM1-18	WM1-18
Tyre size		
Front	3.00-18	3.00-18
Rear	3.00-18	3.00-18

Dimensions

	D5	D7
Seat height	29½in (737.5mm)	30in (750mm)
Wheelbase	51in (1275mm)	51in (1275mm)
Weight (inc 1 gallon of petroil)	228lb (103.6kg)	232lb (105.5kg)

Performance (extracted from published road test data)

	D5	D7
Top speed	56mph (90km/h)	56mph (90km/h)
Acceleration	Standing quarter-mile in 24 secs	Standing quarter-mile in 27 secs
Braking distance from 30 mph to rest.	34ft	33ft
Fuel consumption	150mpg @ 30mph (1.9ltr/100km @ 48km/h), 112mpg @ 40mph (2.5ltr/100km @ 48km/h)	136mpg @ 30mph (2.1ltr/100km @ 48km/h), 125mpg @ 40mph (2.25ltr/100km @ 48km/h)

Keeping Up With the Competition – The D7

Hire purchase fuelled the late 1950s boom for motorcycle ownership, but of the 330,000 new two-wheelers registered in Britain in 1959 over half were scooters. The clean-cut Italian Lambretta and Vespa machines stood in sharp contrast to the traditionally oily British motorbikes. The latest Bantam did not exactly cut a dashing figure in comparison, with its ugly frame lugs, parts that needed a spanner and bolted-up brackets. The market was less inclined to accept exposed chains and oily widgets. The fashion was definitely for slim lines and curvy enclosures to hide all the mechanical mess. The Bantam needed a facelift. After just one year, the 1958 D5 Super was consigned to history; as a result, it is one of the more elusive models today.

There was a marked emphasis on new styling at BSA in late 1958. Unit construction was the trend for the future as the company unveiled the new OHV 250, the C15. The 'Ceefer' set the trend for sleekly valanced fenders, softer-profiled body parts, and a one-piece headlamp nacelle with integral upper fork shrouds. The style was applied upwards to the highly successful 650cc A10 Golden Flash, and all the way down to the Bantam. The new style had all the hallmarks of the irascible, assertive and egotistic Edward Turner, and his sacred Triumph twins. The work itself was carried out by Turner's long-suffering lieutenants; the genius himself hardly ever bothered to venture on to BSA design territory, let alone involve himself with something as lowly as the Bantam.

Designated the 175cc Bantam D7 Super, in a nod to its 7.5bhp output, the new model introduced for the 1959 catalogue. There was a completely new frame and new shapes made it neater and more compact. While it was certainly much smarter than its predecessor, BSA's design engi-

Michael Martin in the early days of 175cc development at Redditch. This was a three-speed engine; four-speed gear clusters were yet to arrive. (Courtesy Michael Martin)

Better looks Better performance Better features

a new **BSA** *175cc*

Bantam Super

The D7 Super was announced in late 1958. The smarter, sleeker 'pretty-bike' style was typical for BSA at the time. (Courtesy Steve Foden, BSAOC)

neers had shunned the spot-welded, pressed-steel concepts that had become popular on the continent and the D7 remained a true little-big motorbike with a proper tubular frame and real forks. It had a cleaner rear seat and suspension sub-frame and a neat compartment for the toolbox/battery joined by a central panel that masked the frame rear down tube. Hydraulically damped forks, a shorter version of the new C15 type, were fitted and the brakes were further increased to 5?in (137.5mm) diameter by 1in (25mm) wide. A fixed nacelle headlamp, housing a circular speedometer and the lighting switch, added to the crispness of the new look.

The engine, virtually that of the D5, was given a new flat-top piston carrying three rings instead of the previous two and a gudgeon pin located by wire-type circlips. The motor also came in for some cosmetic treatment. The Edward Turner influence led to an extra cover for the generator and clutch mechanism, giving the power unit a smooth and symmetric egg shape on both sides. The new left-hand outer cover had the motif 'Super' scrawled all over the surface.

One of the most interesting features of the D7 was the use of colour. The bright Royal Red body, red mudguards and a central battery/toolbox compartment, and an ivory panelled tank,

Launched at the October 1958 Earls Court show, the 175cc D7 Super quickly attracted potential Bantamites. (Courtesy Steve Foden, BSAOC)

contrasted well with the black frame, forks and other cycle parts, painted according to BSA's adopted policy. It made the old Mist Green, pastel grey and maroon schemes look very dull and dreary.

On the open road, the D7 benefited from the flexible and easygoing manners of the flywheel generator engine housed in a more modern hydraulically damped frame. The days of canvas screens, legshields and bulb horns had gone. The D7 was always a safe bike, with or without L-plates. The revised swing-arm frame handled well, adjustable footrests were a blessing and the brakes were able to deal with the extra weight and performance.

The model had its detractors, however. They regretted the fact that the simplicity and charm of the old 125 and 150 types had gone, and felt

A publicity 'white sheet' photograph of the 1958 show-prepared D7 Super with models posing in respectable non-oily apparel. (Courtesy Steve Foden, BSAOC)

It's a beauty! The 1960 175cc Bantam Super. (Courtesy Steve Foden, BSAOC)

that the Bantam had become too flabby in its middle age. Compared with 216lb for the short-lived D5 and just 153lb for the old D1, the D7 weighed 224lb. The styling was not to everyone's taste either. The opposition at BSA to anything demonstrating Triumph influence was shared by enthusiasts. The nacelle-fork shrouds, especially on the top-of-the-range 500 and 650cc twins, were often ripped out and replaced with a sepa-rately mounted headlamp and a set of go-faster rubber gaiters.

Some of the more subtle changes applied to the D7 caused certain headaches. In an effort to reduce costs, some tampering with the gearbox mainshaft splines made the three-speed assembly weaker than the original D1 cluster – and on an engine of almost twice the power output! Adding to the risk of stripped gears caused by hasty downward gear changes, the change mechanism also had the habit of coming apart or jumping out of gear when the bike was harshly ridden. The gearbox parts were not easily interchangeable with those on earlier models. The extra power burden also told on the woodruff key, which fixed the generator flywheel to the engine mainshaft, with very noisy and expensive consequences.

Neither was the new frame without misdemeanours, although this did not manifest itself until many thousands of miles had been completed. The swing arm consisted of a case-hardened spindle running in thin-wall, steel-backed bronze bushes. With regular use of the grease gun, the arrangement lasted well. However, over a period of time, minute particles of hard spindle embedded themselves in the soft bronze and acted as an effective grinding paste to wear away the spindle. The telltale sign (apart from an obvious amount of play in the swing arm) was the

bike getting stuck in one direction, especially if the front and rear wheel were straddling the central white line on the road!

Issues of supply and demand meant that various electrical specifications continued to vex Bantamites. The earlier D7 Supers and D7 Silvers from 1965 on could still be supplied with AC 'direct' lighting using a Wipac two-coil generator, and many were, right up until the end of 1966. Without the engine running there would be no lights but people were still likely to buy the bike. Many tried to improve illumination by fitting a 30/24W bulb instead of the specified 24/24W, and wondered why the rear lamp blew. The biggest problem when night riding was the dreaded black pause when operating the dipswitch. The modern remedy is to fit a clipper diode.

The D7 cycle parts could be irritating. The toolbox/battery covers were fixed by hollow coin-slot screws, which often refused to find their

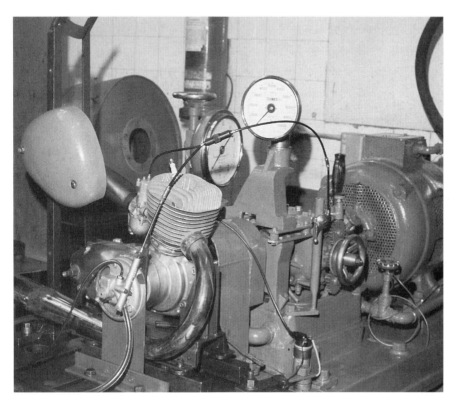

Left *An 'oil pump' Bantam engine on test in Redditch. Work on a direct-lubrication engine was well advanced by the mid-1960s. Although it was technically successful, cost constraints prevented it from reaching production. (Courtesy Michael Martin)*

Opposite *The cosmopolitan appeal of the Bantam is evident in this publicity shot. The model is a 1965 D7 De-Luxe, the first type to be fitted with the jelly-mould tank. (Courtesy Alistair Cave)*

*The D7 De-Luxe on show at Earls Court 1964. A BSA
salesman is out to impress John Huet, the main BSA distributor
for Dublin, Ireland. (Courtesy Mick Walker)*

mating thread without a bit of thumping and
hammering. The seat was still a nuisance to
remove, being clamped by the upper rear damper
bolts. Fortunately, D7 owners were spared the
worst horror of the C15, as the rear hub, brake
drum and sprocket were combined into a one-
piece casting. The Bantam rear sprocket was riveted to the hub making it viable to replace when
worn.

Over the next few years, the D7 received
scarce attention other than new colour options.
For 1960, Sapphire Blue, Fuchsia Red or black

were turned out. In 1962 the once-proud Bantam cockerel tank transfers were cast aside. Fuel
tanks now carried red, acrylic, pear-shaped
badges, an established feature found on larger
machines. Chrome-plated tank panels to go with
the new badges were classed as an extra. On the
technical side, the con-rod little-end bush was
replaced by a Torrington needle roller bearing
and there were plans to uprate the gearbox.

Chris Vincent was helping out with development at this time. He road tested a D7 with a
four-cog cluster, but it kept falling apart; it was
probably the only Bantam on which you were
guaranteed to find neutral – all seven of them!
Progress was not helped when the test bike was
wiped down the road by a large lorry. Vincent
came through the ordeal unscathed but the

crumbled remains of the Bantam disappeared into the famous Small Heath black hole for failed experiments and lost causes. The D7 and the potential of the Bantam would have to remain hampered by the limit of three widely spaced gears for some time yet.

Two years later the silencer shape was revised, with a plain conical end adopted instead of the small fishtail. Magnetic-type speedometers were introduced at this time as components were cheapened to a base-level price. The workings were sealed in a cylindrical canister with a chrome-plated, swaged on bezel with an instrument face that was grey rather than black. Hall effect magnetic speedos were less tolerant of vibration and British weather. The viewing glass misted up after a shower and sometimes packed up completely if excess water was allowed to penetrate.

In late 1964 the basic D7 Super was joined by a De-Luxe version. It was the first to have a new-style 'jelly-mould' fuel tank, a slim, kidney-shaped affair with round silver star acrylic badges, recessed knee sections, acres of bright chrome plating and a central filler cap. The fancy new tank shape meant a slight loss in fuel capacity, from 2 to 1.9 gallons. For £141 the De-Luxe came with a truly luxurious Flamboyant Red finish, achieved by applying the base colour on to a silver layer to create a deep metallic sheen. The mudguards and side panels were picked out with white lining applied by a highly skilled coach painter and his sable brush.

In March, Bob Currie, Midland Editor for *The MotorCycle*, tried out the latest round of changes and spent a day on the latest D7 Super. His opinion was that if you 'get it cracking…it feels as light as a ballet dancer – yet solid with it. This is, you feel, a remarkably durable little bike, capable of shouldering oodles of hard work without complaint.' According to Currie's report, the basic D7 was good for a steady 50mph (80km/h), could do it all day and still return a fuel consumption mpg in the high 90s (around 2.75ltr/100km).

Andrew Dawson was a trainee land surveyor in 1964. He was 19 and had managed to scrape enough money together to go out a buy a brand new Sapphire Blue and chrome D7 Super. He learnt to ride it on a neighbour's driveway and after three months he passed his test. 'I found out soon enough that three gears never seemed to be right,' he recalls. 'Going up hills in Kent you were either buzzing in second or slogging in third. With a new motor the advice given was to load the engine lightly and keep it spinning so I accepted that hill climbing, for the first 500 to 1,000 miles was going to be fairly slow.' Once running-in was complete, Dawson found that the D7 Super cruised comfortably at 45–50mph (70–80km/h) with an all-out maximum (with everything shaking) of just under 65mph (100km/h). He eventually managed over 12,000 miles (19,000km) and, apart from one brief blip when the emergency start came to his rescue, the D7 never went wrong. However, one long and irritating saga ruined his purchase. He got through eight sets of forks. Every 200 miles, oil would surge out of the top seals and the bike had to go back to the dealer again and again. It even went back to BSA's service department but the problem persisted. BSA even sent out a technical engineer to see it, but he declared (in a strong Brummy accent) that he could not understand it. The Bantam was soon traded in for an Ariel Arrow and the problem with the D7 remains a mystery to this day.

The standard D7 Super was eventually dropped for 1965 and replaced in the programme by the D7 Bantam Silver. This had the same specification as the De-Luxe but with the minimum of chrome plating and mod cons, to offer the most basic cheap and cheerful Bantam. Colours for the D7 De-Luxe were extended to Flamboyant Blue with white lining while the D7 silvers were more often finished in the paler Sapphire Blue with silver sheen tank panels. All models had the jelly-mould tank and round plastic silver star badges. The super inscription on the left-hand engine cover was deleted and replaced by a more modest fluted piece of sculpture. The latest D7 De-Luxe also had an improved dual seal with pillion strap and re-profiled handlebars with ball-end levers. (This may have been introduced

The NEW Silver Bantam
Model D7

Lowest in price, sky-high in value! Penny-for-penny, mile-for-mile, the new Silver Bantam is unbeatable in the 175 cc. market. Attractive new finish — petrol tank in Sapphire blue with polychromatic silver panels; mudguards and headlamp in polychromatic silver; side covers in Sapphire blue; frame and forks black.

Above *'Oyl giv it foyve!' Publicity picture of a 1965 175cc D7 Bantam Silver, likely to have been taken on the BSA Sports and Social Club sportsfield at Small Heath, Birmingham. The 'model' was probably one of the office girls. The Bantam advertising budget did not run to much in those days! (Courtesy Alistair Cave)*

Left *The D7 Silver offered the most affordable and basic 50mph motorcycle.*

because the inadequate centre stand meant that most Bantams were parked leaning against the wall!)

As ever, the electrical apparatus continued to confound anyone who ventured beyond the outer cover. The basic Super was always available with the lighting supplied straight from the flywheel generator. Then came an uprated version of the rectified system to give stable lighting and a trickle charge to a battery. Both of these types had one switch on the headlamp shell. The latter

eventually gave way to a system with a separate ignition coil mounted under the seat and fed from a trickle-charged battery. Lighting was supplied straight from the generator – again, no engine running, no lights. This version had two switches in the headlamp with the ignition switch having an emergency start facility. All three systems were in production at one time and riders and service technicians had a hard time sorting it out.

Living with a Bantam

The most perplexing routine involved with running a Bantam was the matter of mixing oil into petrol. Those who were experienced with two-stroke motors understood the drill, but new owners had to be constantly reassured that the correct amount of oil in the fuel tank was of paramount importance. The fuel tank filler cap included a tubular measure and the cap was inscribed with suitable brands of oil, and recommended two measures for each imperial gallon of petrol. Correct mixing would

ensure the long life of the bike but there was an extraordinarily wide range of interpretations among Bantamites.

Despite carrying out high-mileage testing, BSA's Redditch experimental department could never allow for the strange habits of Bantam owners. Straight grade oils were the norm in the early years and, if a bike was

continued overleaf

Living with a Bantam meant never having to wait for a bus again (except when it went back to the dealer for another warranty repair!) (Courtesy Steve Foden, BSAOC)

Typical Bantam 'information centre': no oil warning lamp, no neutral indicator and nothing much else to worry about. The 70mph speedometer was typical for the 150cc models. (Owen Wright)

Dirty work: de-coking the exhaust was made easier when detachable baffles were introduced in 1953. (Owen Wright)

continued from page 87

allowed to stand for any length of time, the oil would sink to the bottom of the tank. Consequently, the engine would at first run oil-rich and then with none, with predictable results. Eventually, self-mixing '2T' oils became available although many owners still swore by nothing but straight SAE 40 grade. One owner ran his D1 on the sump drainings of an Austin A30, apparently without any problems. The correct drill was to put the petrol in first, then the oil, and to swish and shake the bike until they were mixed correctly.

The correct fuel to lubricant ratio was 20:1, or 16:1 for running in a new machine. Later models specified 24:1 and modern two-stroke oils allow 32:1. Some owners would invariably over-do the oil 'just to make sure'. In the most extreme cases, the bike would emit clouds of smoke. A seriously weakened petrol/air mixture would cause mis-firing, a fouled plug or pinking.

Most roadside garages had oil dispensers operated by a hand pump, set to give the correct dollop of oil for each imperial gallon of standard petrol. Some had self-mixing pumps to fulfil the high demand from the petroil-fed two-stroke engines in Bond Minicars, Villiers-powered motorcycles, autocycles and mopeds. In fact, most Bantam owners carried a bottle of two-stroke self-mixing oil in a canvas bag, along with a pair of spare spark plugs, and simply remembered the formula of 1 filler capful for 4 pints of petrol. However they mixed their petroil, its acrid aroma clung to the back of the throat and accompanied Bantam owners everywhere.

The oils used in the earlier days were high in sulphur content and, after a few thousand miles, the exhaust system became encrusted with carbon. As performance

Typical D3–D5 rear brake detail showing rear chain adjusters and brake linkage. (Owen Wright)

started to wane, de-coking became a necessary and regular chore. It involved taking off the cylinder head and using a soft scraping tool to remove the carbon deposits from the top of the piston, cylinder head and the exhaust port. Cleaning the exhaust pipe and silencer was a harder and dirtier job. A packet of soda crystals, mixed in a bucket of water, was poured into the pipe and silencer. Left overnight the solution would break down the harder layers of carbon, and then the Bantamite would have to set to work with a wire brush. Precautions had to be taken to stop the caustic soda coming into contact with any chromium plating. An oozing black concoction of soot mixed with oil usually coated the home mechanic from head to foot. Post-1954 Bantams had removable silencer baffles, which made the job easier.

Re-greasing the rear chain was another important ritual. A chain was considered to be defunct if it had 'stretched' by more than 2 per cent. For example, if the 117 pitches of ?in pitch Renolds chain measured 58?in when new, it should have been thrown away if it had grown by more than an inch. Many Bantam chains were left to hang like a washing line and rarely saw anything more than a quick squirt of ordinary household 'Three-in-One' oil, but the correct procedure was to take off the chain completely, allow it soak in paraffin overnight and then hang it up to dry. The chain was then soaked in a bowl of oil, the excess was wiped off, then the chain was re-assembled. The ultimate lubrication involved boiling the chain in Link-Lyfe, a very effective grease that clung

continued overleaf

continued from page 89

inside the rolling elements and plates, kept out water and vastly extended the life expectancy of the chain. The drawback was the putrefying smell of the boiling vat of grease.

Changing the gearbox oil was another charade. The centre-stand cross-brace tube was directly underneath the gearbox drain plug, so when the plug was unscrewed, nothing could stem the torrent of black oil that would gush from the gearbox, hit the tube and spew all over the ground. Filling the gearbox with fresh oil was equally messy. The average funnel would not fit because of the close proximity of the filler plug to the back of the cylinder. As late as the 1980s, a piece in the BSA owners' jour-

Front brake detail of D1–D5 models. The front wheel was quite easy to remove but required a certain knack. (Owen Wright)

nal *The Star* lamented the fact that 'Man has run a mile in under four minutes, split the atom and landed on the moon but only now has he (Halfords) devised a funnel small enough to fill a Bantam gearbox with oil!' In fact, a small funnel bought at a garden centre would serve the purpose, at least on the early 'pineapple'-cylinder D1 Models. The larger fin-cylinder barrels issued from 1954 made the job more difficult.

Tyres would generally last for about 20,000 miles (over 30,000km). Dunlop Universals were the original factory fitting, a fairly hard-wearing tread that did a good all-round job. Dunlop K70 Gold Seals came along later. Popular replacements tended to be Avon Speedmaster (or 'suicide master', in Bantam speak), ribbed front and block tread rear. Whatever was re-fitted, a new rear tyre exposed one of the Bantam's most enduring idiosyncrasies – the centre stand was suddenly too short! Endless usage wore away the tubular feet until the stand was rendered useless. Welding on new feet was tricky, because the central footrest bar tended to become so bent and corroded. The only course of action was to weld the feet in-situ, risking setting fire to the machine. Because of the inadequacy of the centre stand, bikes were often leant against a wall or a lamppost, resulting in the plastic handlebar grips being torn and gouged and the bars themselves bent and distorted, as well as unseen damage to the steering headstock cups and cones.

Living next door to a Bantam owner meant that you would have a pretty good idea of the comings and goings of your neighbour. What were the plug suppressers for again?

On early models the engine was stopped by shutting off the throttle to its stop, which meant keeping some revs up when waiting at traffic lights or a junction. On later models with an ignition switch, a monobloc carburettor with a throttle stop screw was supposed to let the engine idle. The later Amal carburettors were not ideal for two-strokes, however, and, like most other equipment, had been built down to a price. Variances in temperature meant that the bike would either cut out when cold or stand there screaming when hot.

After changing hands a dozen times the average worn-out Bantam had no street value. Owners would scrimp and save, make do and mend, sometimes to the point of cutting the grooves of a worn-out tyre down to the canvas with a hacksaw blade. The writing was on the wall when a plastic leopardskin seat cover (an obligatory fitting in the early 1960s) had been fitted, the wiring was held together with sticky tape and the once-pristine enamel was daubed with Finnigans Hammerite (usually in Green Metallic). Another Bantam was about to die.

Above *A 1954 D1 Plunger with a dual seat (probably a later addition). Note the typical repair of the centre-stand feet! (Courtesy Mick Walker)*

Right *On the island of Tonga, a man's wife, mother-in-law and sister can all get a ride courtesy of a modified BSA Bantam! (Courtesy Alistair Cave)*

BSA

175 BANTAM

PASTORAL

MODEL D7

BSA Pastoral models are made for hard work on sheep farms, cattle stations, prairie land or veldt where roads are non-existent. Developed from the hard experience gained in trials, scrambles and moto-cross events, these sturdy, reliable machines are the untiring "workhorse" of the modern farmer.

Further Applications for the Bantam Engine

A number of boardroom policy changes in the early 1960s were to affect Small Heath's efforts to produce motorcycles on an economic scale. The manufacture of large-capacity twins was assigned to the Triumph Meriden factory and everything else was shifted to BSA. The Ariel plant at Selly Oak had been scaled down and all production, along with spares and other outstanding obligations, was absorbed into BSA. This meant that Small Heath had to grapple with an ever-increasing array of model types, including the Bantam's arch rival, the Triumph Tiger Cub, various scooters, the monocoque-chassis Ariel leader and Arrow two-stroke twins as well as BSA's own existing range. The Bantam was one of the few models that could be part of a planned build programme, with frames, engines and all necessary bits and pieces being prepared in such a way as to allow an unhindered assembly run. For General Works Manager Alistair Cave, and his team of production planners and engineers, the Bantam was a godsend, although at times certain developments threatened to suck even that model into the increasing chaos.

In 1962, BSA had announced another lightweight, the 75cc OHV Beagle, a pressed-steel, open-framed job with a cantilever-mounted engine. In terms of style, trend and intention, the Beagle pre-dated the Yamaha FSIE of the 1980s. However, it failed due to a premature release, the poor build quality of the initial models and a notorious reputation for devouring big-end bearings. The Beagle had an ugly sister called the Ariel Pixie – a silly name that offended many a follower of the Ariel 'iron horse'. With its feeble 50cc engine and a disastrous press-tin frame, the Pixie was doomed from the start. In an effort to save something from the dis-

aster, both frames were fitted with a 175cc Bantam engine. The Beagle version, probably the more viable of the two, never got beyond a prototype; on the other hand, sanction was given at the highest level to stock up on frame pressings for the Pixie, even though virtually no testing and development had been carried through. Pallet loads of pressed-steel piece-parts began to occupy various corners of the plant. Fortunately, Peter Glover, working his way up the ladder from Service Engineer to International Sales Manager, was told to clear up the factory space, 'and get rid of what you think might be junk!' When he saw all the clutter, he called in a scrap merchant and consigned the whole lot to oblivion. Without a doubt, Peter Glover served British motorcycling, BSA and the reputation of the Bantam well that day.

The Bantam engine found another application when a range of BSA-Triumph 250 and 175cc scooters was announced in 1959, in an attempt to challenge the domination of Lambretta and Vespa. The BSA version was badged under the 'Sunbeam' name and the smaller version used a power unit closely based on the 175cc Bantam unit, but with revised internals to accept fan cooling and a built-in four-speed gearbox. Sadly, it was too late to wean customers away from the strongly established Italian brands. The BSA Sunbeam faded away during 1965, along with the rest of the scooter boom.

There were very few people employed at BSA who fully understood two-strokes, which probably accounted for the cautious progress thus far. Ed Wright was given a 'mod' to do when he worked as a draughtsman at Small Heath, working under Chief Designer Ernie Webster. The job was to alter the dimensional tolerances of the bronze small-end bush. The drawing had already been changed ten or twelve times over the years and now Wright was being asked to revert it back to its original status! No one could be certain either if the Bantam was actually making any profit. The parts were built down to a low price and the margins were small. If anything, the profits was made in the sales of spares, of which BSA produced copious amounts.

Opposite *The origins of the Bushman model and a consequent interest in off-road motorcycling started with the BSA Bantam D7 Pastoral, which was targeted at farmers throughout the Commonwealth. (Courtesy Steve Foden, BSAOC)*

Perhaps the most significant victim of cost control was the development of an autolube system based on a method used by Suzuki. By using a proportional metering valve controlled from the throttle twist-grip, the precise amount of oil could be fed to the engine at any speed. At least one prototype machine fitted with such apparatus had successfully clocked up thousands of miles during 1964. The concept would have put an end to mixing 'petroil' and would surely have given the Bantam a whole new lease of life, but it was scuppered by the harsh realities of material and labour costs, and the economics of mass-producing a low-profit margin motorcycle.

The End of the D7

By the mid-1960s the best Bantam years had gone. The D7 had enjoyed a long and successful run and the attractively priced D7 Silver had made its contribution by bringing in bundles of fresh orders. The D7 was the version that came nearest to establishing some credible sales in the lucrative US market, where it was called the '175 Flash'. There was also a special 'Trail Bronc' version with a prancing white horse motif carried on the gas tank. It was intended for dirt roads and cross-country fun. Unfortunately, the Americans never liked the idea of sloshing two helpings of oil into a gasoline tank and both versions of BSA's Wild West two-stroke had few takers. In the Australian outback the idea of an off-road Bantam had a more practical value. There it was known as the 'Pastoral' and it came in very useful for mustering sheep. A consignment of D7 Trials for the export market were produced in the hope of re-kindling a factory-built off-road competition bike but, along with the other limited-issue variants, it lacked the commitment and support to enjoy any success.

Throughout 1965 another re-design was on the stocks. The Bantam had been allowed to languish with outdated electrical equipment, and there was a never-ending demand for more snap, precision and performance, so some fresh ideas were needed if BSA was to keep producing

The 175 Bantam Pastoral as seen in an overseas-only catalogue in 1963. (Courtesy Steve Foden, BSAOC)

Dual seat standard.
Single seat as shown,
optional.

BSA

175 BANTAM PASTORAL

model D7

Powered by a 175 c.c. two-stroke engine of proved design and reliability, the Bantam D7 Pastoral model with its sturdy frame and hydraulic suspension will give years of trouble-free service anywhere in the world.

A 1966 D7 Super – the last of the flywheel magneto models. (Owen Wright)

thousands of cheap lightweights to pay its over-heads and to encourage more young riders to choose a BSA.

History has not been kind to the D7 and the series has been left with a reputation for being uninspiring and rather bland. The electrical system often let the side down but fortunately there were some heroes among these models. In January 1987, *Classic Bike* magazine published an extensive travelogue telling how Julian Preece rode his 1966 D7 on a 10,000-mile (16,000-km) journey to Central Africa and back via Eastern Europe and the Middle East. The bike was already classed as a clapped-out rust heap when he departed in the early 1980s for his eight-month epic. He never expected to reach Dubrovnik in the former Yugoslavia, but against all expectations the bike carried on through Turkey, Syria, Israel and into Egypt, eventually reaching Bangui in the Central African Republic. The homeward leg northwards went through Zaire and on to Algeria and the South of France, via the steamer, before the long ride back to England. The bike was a virtual wreck, with parts that had shattered, broken, bent, fallen off and worn away. Some had even been pinched, but still the D7 went on, proving that a Bantam would run with faults that would stop a modern Japanese machine in its tracks.

By 1966, with the scooter craze virtually over, opposition from AMC and various Villiers-pow-ered 'constructor's bikes' seldom threatened the supremacy of the Bantam. However, a massive and all-consuming power was developing on the other side of the world that threatened to devour all that lay in its path.

In 1963 the Honda Corporation of Japan opened one of its first European manufactur-ing plants, in Belgium, and Soichiro Honda announced his intentions: 'I regard the sales potential for Honda two-wheelers in Europe as limitless.' In 1948, when the BSA Bantam made its first public showing, Mr Honda was fitting surplus two-stroke engines into old bicycle frames. The 50cc Honda step-thru Super Cub, launched in 1958, went on to con-quer the market for utilitarian lightweights at the expense of mopeds and scooters. In its first year alone, 24,000 units were made, followed by 167,000 in 1959 and 800,000 by 1962. Just six years later, Soichiro Honda would person-ally ride the ten-millionth Honda motorcycle from one of his many production lines. The days of the tried and trusted Bantam were ebbing away, dwarfed by the colossus of never-ending Japanese production.

4 Swan Song (The D10, D14/4 and B175 Models)

The swinging sixties saw the birth of flower power and a seemingly never-ending party. Limitless reserves of oil discovered in the North Sea meant that everyone was going to be rich and no one need ever work again. The reality was that there were strikes at the docks and at the British Motor Corporation, and the Labour government was racked by one economic crisis after another. Establishment figures, traditions and social institutions were attacked on all sides. Dr Beeching took his axe to Britain's railways and nothing was sacred, least of all a British motorcycle industry propped up by the perennial BSA Bantam.

Competition from the Far East

In the mid-1960s, in many a British town and village, local lads began to be seen riding not a Beesa, but an 'Onda'. According to the unitiated, a Japanese bike would probably be fabricated from lengths of bamboo, lashed together with rope, with a paper lantern for a headlamp. In truth, the Honda 90s that began to be seen on Britain's roads were neat, with cables routed and tucked away. The switchgear was slick, handlebar mirrors and flashing indicators were standard, and the bike ran cleanly, like a sewing machine. Moreover, contrary to expectations, it was not cheap and tinny, and it never seemed to break down. The world of motorcycling would never be the same again.

Motorcyling in the mid-1960s had been going through a bad patch. The traditional oily British big banger had acquired a notorious 'greaser' image. Although it was hardly the bike of choice for the Hell's Angels, the Bantam was tarred with the same brush. The Japanese imports were new and exciting, with flashy colour schemes and engines that did not cough, splutter or spew oil. With electric starting and full accessories fitted as standard, the average Japanese lightweight was simply streets ahead of its British counterpart; any annual model update on a British bike still amounted to little more than moving a switch from one side of the headlamp to the other.

A consignment of crates arrived at BSA one day, containing Japanese motorcycles, including a Honda 250cc 'Dream' and a 125cc single. The merchandise was directed to various corners for a covert examination and assessment. Bert 'Mr BSA' Perrigo, who gave long and loyal service to BSA both as an expert rider and as Chief Development Engineer, rode the 'Dream' around the test track and ran out of superlatives to describe it. Alistair Cave, Small Heath General Works Manager, prepared a report that stated that the cost of machine tools to meet the standard of the cam gears found in the Honda would exceed his annual machine tool budget for the entire factory.

Jack Dyson, who had worked in various departments at Redditch since de-mob in 1946, had the job of stripping down a Japanese motorcycle when he was working in the development section at Redditch. A group of engineers came down to see the entrails that had been extracted from the crankcases. As they sifted through the various parts, the atmosphere became solemn. As they inspected the incredibly intricate and accurate die-castings there were gasps of disbelief.

While a cloud of deep and darkening concern must have descended upon BSA, the official line given was that Japanese motorcycles would present no threat to future operations. However,

Right *Early 1950s advertising was at pains to make the Bantam socially acceptable. (Courtesy VMCC Library)*

Below *A D10 Supreme in black and chrome with the original white lining in the mudguards and side panel. Bantam owners had to supply their own pieces of wood when parking on grass! (Owen Wright)*

The World-Famous **BSA BANTAM**

In 1953, owning a D1 Bantam offered unlimited travel but taking a casual weekend trip down to the French Riviera was perhaps pushing it a bit! (Courtesy VMCC Library)

The final version of the D1 finished in Ruby Red and cream. A BSA dictate issued in 1958 ordered all frames to be black. The dual seat and pillion footrests were an extra. (Courtesy Steve Foden, BSAOC)

Left This fully restored 1968 D14/4 Sports in Flamboyant Red has the correct racing seat, flyscreen and high-level exhaust. (Owen Wright)

Opposite The D1 Bantam was built by ladies and ridden by ladies. By 1952, it really was everybody's motorcycle all over the world. (Courtesy Steve Foden, BSAOC)

...ence, Nurse Joy ...Kean toured 4,05 ...les on her Bantam ...a fuel cost of ...s than £6.

Mr. Wm. Lane, 82 years old, who recently rode from Land's End to John O'Groats, in six days on his Bantam.

Three Adelaide nurses, Juliet Jennings, Ann Bickmore and Mattie Lamont (L. to R.) with their Bantam on which they toured Tasmania, New Zealand and Australia.

Members of the 70-strong London Bantam Motor Cycle Club setting out on their Continental "Over the Alps" tour.

Councillor T. Neville, of Tansley, Derbyshire, a 73-years-old Bantam enthusiast.

Mr. C. Morris, of Victoria Park, Western Australia, who recently completed a 2,000-mile trip on a B.S.A. Bantam, his first machine.

sted
roughout
he World

BSA 125

...ORLD ARE USING B.S.A. BANTAMS

COCK O' THE LIGHTWEIGHTS

BSA BANTAM

The small machine with a **BIG PERFORMANCE**

The 'cock o' the lightweights' was in full cry by 1950. (Courtesy Steve Foden, BSAOC)

Formula Bantam racing offers an affordable introduction to motorcycle racing. All machines must employ the original Bantam diamond frame and engine crankcases. At Mallory Park this machine would be capable of speeds of over 100mph (160km/h). (Owen Wright)

A racing red rooster ready for action in Formula Bantam racing at Mallory Park, 2002. Although many modifications have been made to this machine that was once someone's humble mode of transport, the simplicity and exquisite charm of the 125cc D1 BSA Bantam is still evident. (Owen Wright)

The kids of '58 get to grips with the first Bantam Super. (Courtesy Steve Foden, BSAOC)

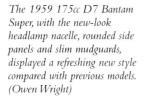

The 1959 175cc D7 Bantam Super, with the new-look headlamp nacelle, rounded side panels and slim mudguards, displayed a refreshing new style compared with previous models. (Owen Wright)

Left *Finished in Sapphire Blue and chrome, the 175cc Bantam Super as it appeared in the 1963 catalogue. (Courtesy Steve Foden, BSAOC)*

Below *The D7 Super and De-Luxe versions as they appeared in an all-colour catalogue for 1965. (Owen Wright)*

175 Bantam Super

This is the seasoned campaigner! Never was so much experience packed into a single model. For more than fifteen years the Bantam has led the lightweight field . . hundreds of thousands have been built, sold and ridden in every country where motorcycles are used.

The Bantam Super illustrated below, is available either with direct lighting or battery lighting and coil ignition. Optional finish is Royal red or Sapphire blue, with chromium tank panels, and black frame and forks.

175 Bantam de Luxe

The latest addition to the popular Bantam series has a re-styled petrol tank, new dual seat, improved handlebar layout, with ball-ended levers, battery lighting and coil ignition and a de luxe finish in flamboyant red, with chromium tank panels, and black frame and forks.

Three

Paul Higgs bought this B175 brand-new in 1970. With 47,000 miles (over 75,000km) on the clock it is still in tip-top original condition. (Owen Wright)

Drive-side view of an all-original 1970 B175 owned from new by Paul Higgs. (Owen Wright)

there was a call for action to take on the challenge of what Prime Minister Harold Wilson had called 'The white heat of technology'.

The New-Generation D10 Series

When the new-generation D10 series was thrust into the world in July 1966 it came in three forms: the basic Silver had painted tank panels and no fancy extras; the Supreme sported a flamboyant paint job, chrome-plated tank and twin mirrors; finally, the biggest surprise of all was a racy-looking Bantam D10S Sports, with a

When it was launched, in 1966, the D10 Supreme had completely revised electrics, powered from a crank-mounted alternator. The contact breaker points were housed behind the circular cover. Cycle parts were generally as the previous D7 De-Luxe, hence the ball-ended levers, pillion grab strap and a 'Modele De-Luxe' motif on the toolbox cover. Note the piece of white card placed discreetly under the engine! (Courtesy Alistair Cave)

humped racing seat, flyscreen, upswept exhaust and, at last, a four-speed gearbox that really worked!

The D10 range came on with a whole new marketing approach designed to appeal to a younger 'get-up-and-go generation'. The images featured sexy models in swimsuits or courting couples on a sunset beach; if BSA's advertising was to be believed, in order to get the girl you had to have a D10 Bantam.

To promote the sporty image, BSA had redeveloped the engine to raise the power output by 40 per cent to 10bhp. The old Wipac flywheel generators, standard fitting since the D1 to D7, had been chucked out for good and replaced by a crank-mounted 60-watt, six-coil alternator providing true coil ignition and battery lighting set-up. A cavity to house a contact breaker set was set into the primary case and protected behind a circular cover with a streamlined fin.

The new D10 breed still looked like a Bantam and had that old familiar three-speed gearbox.

In 1966, Bantams still appealed to the young… even if they were wearing pyjamas. (Owen Wright)

The D10 Silver and Supreme may have benefited from the new engine but otherwise the frame and running gear were much the same as on the 1965 D7 De-Luxe. The Bantam Silver model had its plain blue livery with round silver star tank panels. For £131 17s 3d, it was still good value. For another tenner you could have a Supreme in a flamboyant translucent electric blue, chrome plating and white lining on the mudguards and side panels.

Bob Currie, the Midlands editor for *The MotorCycle*, was closely following BSA's progress and published an extensive special edition road test of a D10 Supreme on 21 July 1966. One of the greatest and most revered motorcycle journalists of his time, Currie produced reports that were crisp, objective and entertaining, and typewritten straight on to paper in one draft. Although noted for his endearing affection and loyalty to Triumph Meriden products, he often betrayed a soft spot for the Bantam:

Livelier than previous models? Of course. With 2 additional ponies in the pot, it has every right to be. But the cunning part is that the additional top-end performance has been achieved without much sacrifice of the characteristic Bantam slogging power. It is an all-purpose runabout, just as happy in city traffic as on the open road… As comfortable as they come, it is a credit to the breed.

On the question of road holding, Currie determined that the D10 handled with easy control and lightness.

Along with the new circular points cover, the D10 was also distinguishable from the earlier D7 by a larger monobloc carburettor and a drum-like air cleaner. The large air filter was in response

Opposite *Exploded view of a D10 series engine. The riveted-on flywheel plates caused serious problems. The drawing shows the three-speed gear arrangement.*

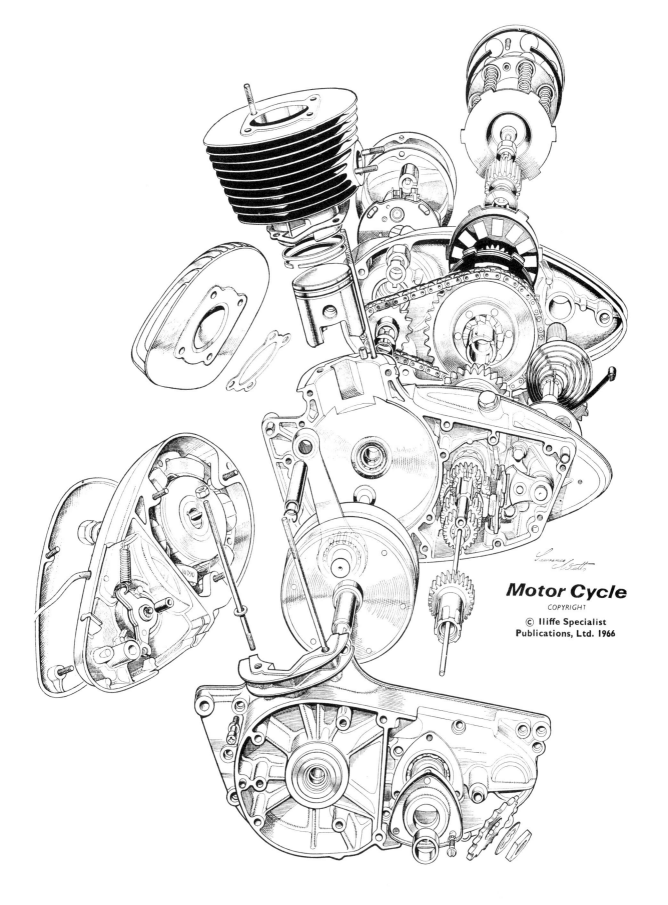

Motor Cycle

COPYRIGHT

© Iliffe Specialist
Publications, Ltd. 1966

to threatened noise regulations; a session of high-speed testing at the MIRA circuit near Nuneaton had found that more din came from the air intake than from the exhaust! Cold starting was also improved. The new carburettor was fitted with a push plunger air strangler that sprang back when released. It was not an easy gadget to operate when you were also trying kick the engine into life but, provided the carb had generous tickling when cold, the additional benefit of coil ignition gave it first or second kick-starting.

There were some things to ponder. The 60-watt electrics were pushing a 30/24-watt head-lamp, which meant that the battery had to be kept in a tip-top state of charge. Gaining access to it meant the usual palaver of getting the dual seat off – slackening off the two upper mounting bolts of the rear dampers and jerking the seat clear. The tired-out three-speed gearbox only became worse with the extra power. On the main roads the D10 could hold a steady 55mph (90km/h) without any harm. There was more available as the motor gave a little more top-end urge. At 60mph (95km/h) for any length of time it started to fluster and Bob Currie recommended a harder plug than the standard Champion N4. To get anything like a smooth and fluent ride through the gears the engine had to be pushed to peak revs when changing up at speeds of 25 and 45mph (40 and 70km/h) respectively, otherwise the slump between gears was depressing.

Clive Bennett, the BSA Development Engineer who had been largely responsible for the D10, revealed some of the thinking behind the updating of the strong BSA brand name: 'To put the D10 into perspective, it is not a super-sports model. My brief was to obtain a reasonable increase in power while keeping the machine within a moderate price bracket. It had to retain its advantages as a tractable utility mount.'

Compared with the D7, power output had risen from 7.5bhp at 4,750rpm to 10bhp at 6,000rpm. The extra 'oomph' was due to crankcase and combustion changes. There was also some riveted flywheel sides to increase crankcase compression and a new style of piston, which was domed instead of flat. Compression

ratio was up too, from 7.4 to 8.65:1, which meant the use of premium-grade fuel and a change to long-reach spark plugs. The combustion chamber hemisphere had actually been slightly reduced with a squish band around the periphery covering some 15 per cent of the piston crown area.

There was also a significant return to a two-ring piston instead of the three-ring job introduced with the D7. 'In the past,' explained Bennett, 'three rings were used to minimize the risk of piston seizure, but the new one is more oval and has more taper, so the need for a third ring is eliminated.' The loss of the third ring enabled a re-think on cylinder-wall porting and improved gas flow. In addition to an increase in height of the exhaust port there was a related increase in revs. Another key area of improvement was a re-design of the inlet port, which was lower in the barrel and took on a kidney shape. The downward kink at the upper profile of the kidney permitted the piston ring to bridge across the port with less risk of becoming trapped in the opening.

With a new engine able to make bigger gasps of puffing and panting, it could deal with a 1in (25mm) choke Amal monobloc and a pancake filter as big as they come. As far as the rest of the motor went, oval-section con-rods were fitted to reduce internal turbulence and allow more oil-mist to settle on the big-end bearing. Another D10 development, often overlooked by Bantam builders, was the insertion of an extra clutch plate.

While Bob Currie was trying out the Supreme, the basement Silver Bantam was doing its best to bring in sales. This no-frills bike kept BSA in the market when the economy continued to slide and in the face of the onslaught from Japan.

Problems with the D10

The D10 story was not without trouble and strife. It developed an infamous warranty and service record and early batches had notoriously leaky engines. The ride itself was certainly harsher and more aggressive, with less flywheel effect than on the old magneto types. Higher engine speeds created more vibration and fatigue. Bolts worked loose and things rattled or disappeared. The flywheel compression plates in particular had a nasty habit of breaking free from their rivets, with very noisy and expensive consequenses. The crankshaft assembly also suffered under the strain and breakages piled up the warranty claims.

Peter Johnson of Letchworth suffered with a sick D10. 'I actually broke the crankpin on my Bantam,' he recalls. 'It started clattering and banging but somehow managed to keep going. I rode it home the last two miles at tick-over. The two broken halves managed to stay engaged! It was a blue D10, I'd paid 85 quid for it. Working for an engineering company I had a new crankpin

The 1966 D10S Sports was very much a part of BSA's 'scene stealers' advertising campaign. (Courtesy Steve Foden, BSAOC)

made, had it case-hardened and ground. After that it was quite a decent bike, and I kept it for three more years.'

D10 Sports Model
With the mainstream bread-and-butter Bantam now following a new direction, the two other versions were to cause plenty of excitement. The D10 Sports model was the first to have a four-speed gearbox. The D10S appealed directly to excitable young men who delighted in hurtling around all day on what sounded like a megaphone full of demented bees. The D10S was unashamedly pretentious but it was fun, and countless machines, from worn-out ex-GPOs to pristine D7 De-Luxes had all been butchered and tuned up by local heroes.

The D10 Sports was also the first to get an Amal 26mm concentric carburettor, the very latest in 1966. *Motorcycle Mechanics* magazine tested

BSA

curtain raisers

BSA's NEW 1967 range of Lightweights set a NEW standard of superb design. Here you have all the comfort and safety of a big motor cycle built round a robust, powerful and easily-maintained 175 cc. engine. Whether you are short or tall you will be at ease on a BSA Model 175.

The New Sportsman (left foreground)

The sportiest 175 cc. anywhere! With four-speed gearbox, upswept exhaust pipe, racing seat, separate chromium headlamp, full-width hubs and chromium plated front forkends, the Sportsman is the ideal choice to the man who wants that extra measure of pleasure from an economical motor cycle. Finished in flamboyant red and chrome.
Western style handlebar optional.

175 Supreme

Offering over 100 m.p.g., with an engine developing 10 b.h.p., the ultra modern styling of the Supreme—with stainless steel handlebar mirrors fitted as original equipment—makes it one of the most desirable models ever produced. Finished in flamboyant electric blue and chrome.

Silver 175

175 cc. of pure unbeatable pleasure. Lowest in price, highest in value. Attractive finish—petrol tank in sapphire blue with polychromatic silver panels; mudguards, headlamp and side covers in sapphire blue; frame and forks black.

You just cannot afford public transport with the Silver 175 now available.

BSA's new D10 Bantam curtain raisers – Silver and Supreme – as they appeared in the 1967 catalogue.

a Sports at Snetterton on a wet and windy morning. *MM* reviewers never shied away from home truths, but the D10S came out rather well, with its exceptional handling and brakes being praised. The reporter did not like the exposed fork shrouds and rear damper springs. The flyscreen and humped rear seat had their uses but the high-level silencer with a heat shield was more for show than anything else. The Sports was the only Bantam so far to have full-width hub brakes; they

looked imposing but proved little better than the standard fitting, which were considered 'adequate'.

The four-speed gearbox went down very well with the test reporter, who recorded a top speed of 62mph (99km/h) and 0 to 50mph in 15.9 seconds. For a standing-start quarter-mile it managed 25.3 seconds, with a terminal speed of 57.6mph (92.15km/h) and, despite all the extra zip, it still returned 90mpg (2.6ltr/100km) on what was reckoned to be a normal all-conditions average.

The D10 Sports looked stunning with its Flamboyant Red paintwork and, in a move that represented the ultimate in 1960s go-faster tat, a strip of black and white chequered tape was stuck along the top of the tank!

The Sportsman came about during a brief and exciting era at BSA when it was under dynamic Managing Director Harry Sturgeon. Sturgeon was a salesman who liked the potent and flamboyant machines, such as the virile, red-blooded 650cc A65 Spitfire, which set the tone during the mid-1960s. He was also a supporter of the fourth

Bantam development so far, the Bushman, which certainly raised a few eyebrows.

The Bantam Bushman
In the mid-1960s, Bantam sales had sunk to levels that made it uneconomic to keep a dedicated engine assembly at Redditch, and production was shifted to Small Heath during the winter of 1965–66. The famous 'Bantam ladies' who once held the world record for motorcycle production (led by the indefatigable Peggy Hutton) had been gradually replaced by male assemblers, due to issues of equal pay, factory legislation and, gener-

The first D10 Bushman in the BSA showroom. It created new branch of off-road motorcycling. (Courtesy Alistair Cave)

ally, changing times. BSA motorcycles were being exported to the USA in ever-increasing numbers and the business was becoming dollar-obsessed. Although the Bantam never really figured in that particular gold rush, it was a proven tough-terrain lightweight. Hundreds of specially modified scramblers, trials and 'mudpluggers', produced by all sorts of owners, ranging from professional builders such as the late Eric Cheney down to the DIY garden-shed mechanic, showed the Bantam's toughness and versatility. The potential of the off-road Australian export Bantam Pastoral had not been realized and there had been no serious intent to build a competition rough-rider since the D1–D3 Competition models of the early mid-1950s.

Peter Glover had been appointed as Assistant International Sales Manager working under Wilf Harrison. The pair were tasked with equalling the number of bikes being sold in the States and to promote a ready outlet for Bantam engines. A possibility of supplying engines to a Portuguese company came to nothing when it was noticed that their manufacturing process consisted of melting down aluminium saucepans to be re-cast as steering head yokes!

Glover eventually came up with the idea of exploiting the Pastoral and taking it a stage further. He produced some sketches showing an imaginative, colourful and attractive bike with increased ground clearance and a trials specification. Alistair Cave arranged for a pair of prototypes based around the current D10. The result was the exciting, dirt-kicking Bantam Bushman trail bike. It immediately found favour with the testers, who enjoyed hours of fun charging up and down the famous hill that formed part of the proving track running around the perimeter of the BSA sports ground. In spite of normal protocol and paper-bound procedures that hampered many adventures and promising developments at BSA, the Bushman somehow managed to make it into production.

The Bushman was a relative rarity in Britain, with most of the 3,500 produced being shipped for export to Australia, New Zealand and Kenya. With its high cradle frame, knobbly tyres and high-rise exhaust pipe, it was one of the first in a new branch of road-legal motorcycles designed for rugged off-road use. Its bright orange and white tank with unique Bushman decals and matching orange side panels made it stand out from the crowd. Its engine specification differed from other D10 models in that it had uprated mainshaft and gearbox bearings. The carburettor was re-jetted to match the overall lower ratios for all four speeds. The rear sprocket was a large 58-teeth item thickened up to take a heavier ?in (12.5mm) pitch, there was a .335in roller chain and most were fitted with direct lighting.

Developments and Missed Opportunities

The D10 series had been a significant development in the Bantam story even if its raunchy and rorty style went against the grain for established Bantam riders. This was also a time of missed opportunities.

George Todd was already a legendary Bantam tuner, and had spent some time with BSA when he was hired by Chief Development Engineer Bert Perrigo. He immediately started to make a valuable contribution in the R&D department at Redditch, building what could only be described as a 'hot Bantam'. It was full of interesting concepts, although it would have challenged the established methods of mass production by semi-skilled labour. Unfortunately, his expertise in advancing the cause of the two-stroke was wasted on senior management and the Deputy Chairman took a number of people to task over the affair, demanding to know 'Who authorized it?' Glover tried to justify it, stammering about 'the need for effective service after cost…the involvement of pure science…the quest for greater product credibility', but what might have been a significantly important piece of research was scuppered by a Deputy Chairman who took a dim view of extraordinary budgetary activities.

There was a plan to offer flashing indicators as standard but this had to be withdrawn when dealers complained about the extortionate retail price increase of £14. The four-speed gearbox was a success and gained universal approval, but throughout the remaining life of the D10 series,

Another D10 Supreme has passed final assembly inspection and awaits despatch from Small Heath. (Courtesy Alistair Cave)

the Silver and Supreme toiled on with the three-speed version.

In 1956, George Todd published his extensive *Boost up your Bantam* engine tuning notes for a *Motorcycling* feature. BSA later reprinted the article in the form of a technical bulletin and issued it via their service department for would-be Bantam racers. However, in truth, the Bantam had been the least developed of the many derivatives of the DKW RT125. Compared with the efforts being made on behalf of two-stroke motorcycles elsewhere, progress on the Bantam was virtually static. BSA's team of development engineers, including Brian Stonebridge, Bernard Hooper and ex-DKW two-stroke expert Hermann Meier, could make a scrambles Bantam produce

over 100hp/ltr, but their efforts were largely ignored.

Another application for Bantam parts arose during 1966 but it did not involve the engine. The basic D10 rolling chassis was amalgamated with a 200cc OHV single-cylinder Triumph Tiger Cub engine to make the Triumph T20 Bantam Cub. It cost only £165 and offered a first-class all-rounder with a top speed of 65mph. It was a long-overdue marriage between two old rivals and, although it carried Triumph badges, it was built entirely at Small Heath. The Bantam

Cub only lasted for one year but the BSA cycle parts were retained in the more sprightly Super Cub version until the end of 1966.

Engine development at Redditch had been handed over to Michael Martin, brother of the late BSA competition supremo, Brian Martin. Michael Martin had plenty of experience with BSA industrial engines and had contributed to their increasing success. When this sector of the

The official D14/4 handout for 1968. (Courtesy Steve Foden, BSAOC)

business was sold off to Villiers, he was asked to take over Bantam affairs from Clive Bennett. In no time he began formulating plans to further increase the bike's performance rating.

The D14/4

In November 1967, sterling was devalued by 14.3 per cent. 'The pound in your pocket is still the same pound' insisted Prime Minister Harold Wilson, as the economy plunged further downwards. A weaker currency ought to have opened the floodgates to increased sales but, instead, the price

The D14.4 Bantam is the "aristocrat" of the lightweight range. With 4-speed gearbox, a choice of two superb de luxe finishes, black and chrome or electric blue and chrome, and standard equipment which includes ball-ended levers, stainless steel handlebar mirrors, and pillion seat safety strap.

A 175 c.c. engine with 10 : 1 compression ratio and which develops 13 b.h.p., provides real snappy performance at remarkably low running cost. You can confidently expect a performance of well over 60 m.p.h. and a petrol consumption of at least 100 m.p.g. Hydraulically-controlled suspension front and rear for maximum riding comfort. $5\frac{1}{2}$ in. diameter brakes for super stopping power. Petroil lubrication, which means you have to refill with only one type of fuel—no separate oil supply to keep a check on.

In a typical 'Happy Bantam days' publicity picture, an outing for the first production D14/4 in 1968 pauses for a cup of coffee. A cardigan was hardly suitable for weather-beaten Bantamites…and who had to carry that big rucksack? (Courtesy Mick Walker)

of a Bantam to importers had been hiked up by 37 per cent. Peter Glover remembers breaking the news to Snr Geno Ghezzi, BSA's Italian importer:'He fell off his chair and wouldn't speak for about four hours.' In fact, the Bantam had been selling too cheaply and the new price had little effect on existing sales in Italy, or elsewhere.

By the end of 1967, the BSA Bantam was being sold on its reputation and was still as much a part of the British way of life as the shipping forecast. As a brand name it was as familiar as bottled Bass and Swan Vestas. Enough people still pinned their faith on a bike built in Birmingham, expecting a no-nonsense, easy-to-ride, safe-handling bike at the right price. In 1968, the now seemingly immortal Bantam came in for another engine upgrade and cosmetic surgery, to extract just a bit more life out of the old bird.

When the new model was announced as the D14/4, the main thrust of the sales pitch was a further increase power output from 10 to 13bhp

at 5,750rpm. With the compression ratio upped to 10:1 and primary crankcase pressure pumped up with stuffer plates, the extra horses were also found with wider transfer ports, deep inlet tracts and a big fat exhaust pipe of 1 5/8in [[one and five-eighths]] (40mm) diameter. Following the customary fashion to use a model tag to reflect its power rating, the first batch of 600 or so new Bantams were designated as the D13. After their despatch, a serious fear of the number thirteen broke out at BSA and a hasty change to 'D14/4' was arranged. The 13 was rounded up to 14, and the /4 part of the name indicated the greater benefits of the four-speed gearbox, which was now fitted to all versions as standard.

Above *Official factory catalogue picture of a 1968 D14/4S Sports Bantam complete with folding kick-start lever, flyscreen, humped seat and a few other go-faster accessories. (Courtesy Alistair Cave)*

Left *The Bishop of Worcester is thankful for the small mercies of a BSA Bushman. This machine was destined for an African aid project funded in 1968 by the pupils of Kings School, Worcester. Assisting are the Reverend Bernard Hancock, Commander N.R. Corbet-Milward RN and (far right) Mr Martin of W.J. Bladder & Son, the local BSA agents. (Courtesy Alistair Cave)*

Jack Dyson recalls an incident that played a part in the numbers muddle during the final days of the Redditch factory: 'I worked on the development of the D14 engine. It wasn't called the D14 then, we knew it only as a standard Bantam engine. Anyway I did a lot of the work on port modifications, piston design and compression ratios. We had an engine on the brake test one Saturday morning and a number of engineers came down to have a look. They got their slide rules out, got all excited and went running away shouting that it was producing 14bhp. I wasn't too sure, so on the following Monday I checked out the rig and found that one of the test weights had been machined down. It turned out that my mate who'd been testing an industrial engine had thinned it down because he needed a lighter one! By then it was too late, and they were already calling the new Bantam the D14.'

Jack Dyson's corrected figures showed that the test engine was giving 12.6bhp, which probably accounted for certain factions naming the latest Bantam prematurely as 'D13'.

Dyson also produced a trials bike for Mick Bowers, who contested the Scottish Six Days Trial, with a special large-fin alloy barrel and high-level exhaust. He was also handed more of the Bushman project as Small Heath was hard pressed at the time to carry out the work. At the same time, Dave Rowlands achieved a memorable performance by coming second in the Scottish on a Bantam and there was a resurgence of interest in what BSA was planning for the future.

There were three Bantams in the D14/4 family, with the basic Silver dropped from the list. The D14/4 Supreme was barely distinguishable from the previous D10 types, other than by a larger-bore exhaust pipe that almost rubbed against the frame downtube. It was available in either black or Polychromatic Blue with white lining on the mudguards and side panels. The fuel tank was painted in a new 'yin and yang' style with the base colour enveloping the tank badge before curling rearwards.

The D14/4 certainly displayed a little more pep and still held a wide power band with no

The 1969 'Queen of the Road' poses with a D14/4 Supreme. The model has obviously not been wearing a crash helmet! (Courtesy Steve Foden, BSAOC)

low-speed snatch in top gear, and it was all ably assisted by a well-behaved four-speed cluster. The big-bore exhaust with a reverse cone silencer made more of a deep grumble at low speed but on take-off it roared like a VC10. It was great for the younger rider whose fathers still thought that a Bantam was a 'sensible bike'. Others chose to argue that the Bantam had 'outgrown its strength and lost its simplicity', in the words of BSA historian Barry Ryerson.

The new 13bhp motor settled down nicely and would cruise all day at nearly 60mph. Full-throttle 60mph-plus action was pretty hectic, and noisy with it! As if to stave off the immense power increase, heavier fork stanchions were fitted, based on a type that had gone out of fashion some ten years earlier. Another noticeable change was the inclusion of a large paper element air filter housed within the right-hand compartment. The left-hand cover could be removed to gain access to the battery but the aperture was too small and the connecting wires too short to be of any practical use. Despite the use of half-turn cover fasteners, it was still necessary to prise the seat off with a jemmy to get at the battery and electrics. At least the left-side outer engine cover had an access hole, for easier clutch adjustment, which was protected by a rubber blanking plug.

A D14/4S Sports and a D14/4B Bushman complemented the Supreme roadster. These models had beefed-up forks, with long rubber gaiters instead of steel shrouds. The D14/4S Sports was still hoping to win over fashion-conscious young men, with an upswept exhaust leading to a silencer that sat high up above the swing arm. A humped racing seat, flyscreen and exposed rear damper made it look ready for war.

At £130, a D14/4 Supreme was worth considering and the more experienced rider knew the Bantam reputation for economy and reliability – when it came to totting up the bill for fuel, oil, spares, and wear and tear, there was none better. The problem for the Bantam was that a new generation was after the noisiest, meanest bike that their (or their parents') money could buy. The Bantam was hard pushed to satisfy their desires while at the same remaining economically viable. While Japanese products had gizmos galore, BSA also persisted in that infuriating habit of listing essential and useful accessories as extras. Only the truly patriotic clung to the Bantam, often sporting an 'I'm backing Britain' sticker too.

Bantamites!

In the age of the Bantam the world worked at a slower pace. Travel by Bantam was carefree and unstressed. A second-hand D7, a hard-earned essential and the best that many could hope for to get to work or college every week, came into its own as a way of escape. There was also something about the Bantam that attracted adventurers, mild eccentrics and wanderers that the Americans might refer to as 'gasoline gypsies'.

Even BSA was astonished by some of the extensive journeys undertaken by Bantamites. Publicity pictures of homeward-bound riders – 'home' usually being Australia or New Zealand – setting out from Small Heath were a regular feature in the motorcycle weeklies. The most famous Bantam saga is that of Peggy Iris Thomas and her trans-American tour in the early 1950s. Earlier she had appeared in a BSA advert, with her friend P. Beggs on the pillion, about to embark on a mere 4,500-mile (7,200-km) tour of Europe. For the trans-American epic she landed first in Halifax, Nova Scotia, with her D1 Bantam, a bundle of possessions tied down on the rear carrier, and her small Airedale terrier Matelot perched on the tank. Her travelogue *A Ride in the Sun*, published in 1954, charted their progress southwards through the USA and into Mexico. Her beloved Bantam OPE 811 (known as 'Oppy') remained faithful throughout 14,000 miles (22,500km) of highways and dirt roads.

Another lady Bantam rider, Margery Price, would spend hours on the narrow lanes and byways of the Derbyshire Peak District on her faithful D1, singing away at the top of her voice. In the 1960s she wrote *What to sing when you're riding*. Her favourite tune was *The Ride of the Valkyries* sung at the top of her voice. Touring Ireland she could be heard going through all the verses of Slattery's *Light Dragoons*: 'Down from the mountainside came twenty-four platoons, thirty or forty fighting men and a couple of gosoons.' Finally there was an American folk song dedicated to her Bantam: 'Bantam, Bantam, don't you stop, just let your pop go popperty-pop. The chain goes swish and the wheels go round, giddy up, we're homeward bound!' Margery Price received an award in 1997 from the TRF (Trail Riders Fellowship) in recognition of her tireless efforts to maintain the riders' sacred rights of way. She was 84 and still going strong.

In July and August every year Britain's industrial giants of the North and the Midlands allowed thousands of factory workers to escape with two weeks' paid holiday. Ken Goode remembers the adventure he shared with a friend in 1960 when he set out from

continued on page 113

Opposite *Appropriate full plumage for riding a Bantam Cockerel in Papua New Guinea. (Courtesy Alistair Cave)*

Above *Bantamites went everywhere! These two gentlemen rode a D7 to the top of Mount Kilimanjaro (5930m) in Tanzania. (Courtesy Peter Glover)*

Left *In Australia, Bradley Willis was just five years old when he started riding his specially adapted Bantam, built by Mr Willis senior. (Courtesy Steve Foden, BSAOC)*

continued from page 110

Northampton. 'Me and my mate went two-up all the way to Blackpool on a 150 Bantam,' he recalls. 'We met some girls and tried to kip down under the pier until a copper cleared us out. It was a hell of a week.' For Ken and his mate that trip up the A6 must have been an epic: 'We were just two young lads escaping the confines of our small provincial town for the first time and it was like embarking on space travel. A distance of 150 miles probably took us most of the day, battling against a headwind.' The Bantam, loaded up with two youths, would have consumed less than 2 gallons and less than a pint of self-mixing oil to get there. With something like 400lb on board it was sheer cruelty – the suspension would clank, bang and bottom out on every bump and hollow, the engine noise would be terrible, but the old bird would carry on regardless. The world was within their grasp. The Bantam could be parked anywhere, because no one would pinch it – that was the way it was.

Doug Spencer has been a regular visitor to the Western Isles of Scotland, using various modes of transport, including a 1000cc BMW Boxer and a Volvo estate, but there has been nothing to beat the time he went island-hopping on a 125cc Bantam. 'You don't see a country doing 70mph on a motorway. At 30mph on a Bantam you can't help but see everything!' he says. On a student's meagre rations in the late 1950s, it was his first taste of 'international travel'. Greg Pearson was another who headed north on a D7 in the mid-1960s. 'The climb up Shap in pouring rain was the hardest part,' he recalls. 'That three-speed box – it was either groaning away in top or revving like the clappers and it kept jumping out of second!'

Harry Timpson kept a Bantam for years and he was not the only one to be worried by one particular Bantam trait. 'I couldn't stand all that flapping and a-banging when it went down hills,' he says. His journey to work involved a long drop down into a deep valley. 'With the throttle shut and the bike for ever running away with itself, the exhaust would back-fire like a gun going off!' The official rider's handbook warned of the potential risk of engine seizure in such circumstances. A revving engine getting no fuel was also starved of lubrication. Riders were supposed to draw in the clutch occasionally and blip the throttle…

On 8 November 1959, in what was the great boom year for two-wheeler sales, the M1 motorway was opened as far north as Rugby. In an age when there was plenty of cheap 100 octane 5-star petrol, and empty motorways with no speed limits, the M1 was hardly the

In the 1950s the well-heeled Bantamite might have worn a Belstaff 'Black Prince' PVC suit. For most it was an old army jacket and a flat cap turned back to front!

place to ride a Bantam. In the late 1970s, however, Steve and Carol Cotterell swung north at Staples Corner to head for home. 'We went up the M1 motorway with me on a D14/4 and Carol on a D10 Sports,' recalls Steve. 'We got pulled over by the police who were absolutely convinced that we were learners. They were speechless when they realized that we were two mature people, husband and wife, and drove away without saying another word.'

continued overleaf

continued from page 113

'I was always getting stopped,' says Carol. 'I guess they found it hard to accept that a woman was capable of riding a motorbike, even if it was only a Bantam.'

Riding on the vast open road at sustained full throttle on a small two-stroke was living on the edge. In pre-war days two-stroke owners rode with fingers poised on the clutch lever ready to react in the case of engine seizure. It often came without warning; there would be a loud screech and the rear wheel would lock solid. In the motorway age, Bantamites had to learn to live with the anxiety and knew what to do if the engine showed the slightest change of mood. If a D10 or D14/4 series on the motorway was just about viable, the stress and strain could and did take its toll. Carol Cotterell remembers going home from London up the M1: 'Near Rugby I felt the engine go sluggish and tighten up. I got the clutch in quickly and stopped on the hard shoulder. I waited for three-quarters of an hour to let it cool down. Fortunately it wasn't damaged and it never seized up again.'

Another lad keen to escape the confines of his home town was Tony Haywood, who recalls the time he passed his test on 'Chuck': 'When I took my test, the circuit was in a figure of eight, consisting of three side streets and two main roads in Wolverhampton. We didn't get off to a good start, the examiner and I. The eye-sight test was to read a number plate of a Ford Anglia at fifty yards. When

continued on page 116

Opposite *Like father, like grandson: another future Bantamite gets his first ride as Ken Ascott lets his two-year-old grandson 'have a go' on his 1956 D1. (Courtesy Ken Ascott)*

Below *Many miles I've travelled.... Sheila Whittingham takes a breather during a hot August day back in 1965 on her 1950 D1 Bantam MMB 713. (Courtesy Sheila Whittingham)*

John Storey with Project 9, which has seen many sights, from the deserts of Morocco to the icy mountains of Norway. (Owen Wright)

Owen Wright on an ex-GPO D1 in May 1989 attending the British Motorcyclists' Federation rally near Peterborough.

continued from page 112

I said I couldn't see a Ford Anglia but only a Standard Ten, he was a little irate. Next Chuck wouldn't start. "It's only the points," I said, as he gave me five minutes to start it or cancel. I knew all about points by this time, and got it going with one minute to spare.

'I had to do three laps, which included traffic lights. The clutch cable snapped at green. I did some frantic paddling, and stabbing through Chuck's gearbox, till I pulled up outside the test centre to be greeted by the self-satisfied little man, who said, "You 'ad it a bit rough, didn't yer lad?"

'"Oh well," I thought. "I hope I don't get him next time. He can't even tell a Ford from a Standard."

'He surprised me, though. "You've passed, son", he said, "but get that clutch cable fitted by someone who knows how to do it!"'

The Bantam 175

The policy of pushing the Bantam in various directions – tourer, racer and off-road fun bike – was scaled down. In April 1969 the D14/4 was replaced by the Bantam 175. Reducing the number of model types and standardizing on one model was all part of the effort to keep costs to a minimum. Some references call the final Bantam the D175, while others refer to it as the B175. It was another name mess, but the B175 designation, probably instigated by the sales division, seems to be used more frequently.

By the following October, the Bushman and Sports versions were finished for good.

The B175 had a new cylinder head with a vertical and centrally disposed spark plug; all previous Bantams had had the plug slanting backwards. The crankshaft was also unique to the

B175. Mindful of the serious flywheel compression plate problems on the D10, which were still evident on the D14/4 series, the plates were positively fixed with a rolled-in rim lock. The compression ratio was a slightly milder 9.5:1 and other detail changes included a revised gudgeon pin and small-end bearing, and a needle roller bearing added to the clutch chainwheel.

B175 styling in general was that of the D14/4 including the jelly-mould tank that first appeared on the 1965 D7 De-Luxe. Stronger Triumph Sports Cub forks with rubber gaiters were fitted, while the chrome-plated uncovered rear shock absorber springs from the D14/4 series were retained. There were a host of other small changes to the cycle parts, including the silencer-mounting bracket, front brake backplate and torque arm. Colour schemes were black, Flamboyant Red or Blue with the usual white lining on the mudguards and side panels. A decision to implement Unified threads had been made to replace the good old Joseph Whitworth designs, which had been doing sterling service in keeping

A Bushman in final B175 form. Note the central spark plug, restyled cylinder barrel and head. (Courtesy Alistair Cave)

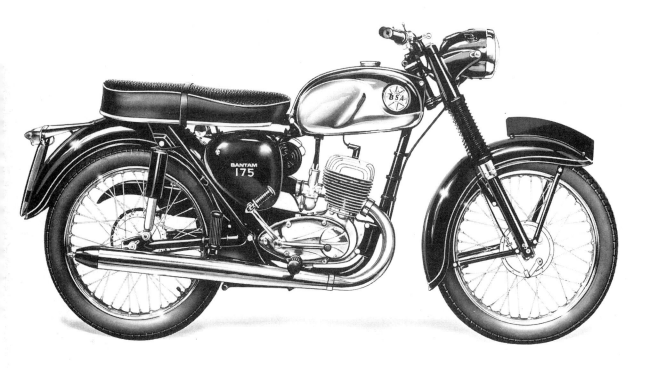

Factory publicity picture of the 1969 Bantam 175, often referred to as the B175. The rear shock absorbers usually had exposed chrome-plated rear springs but the heavier forks with rubber gaiters became standard. (Courtesy Steve Foden, BSAOC)

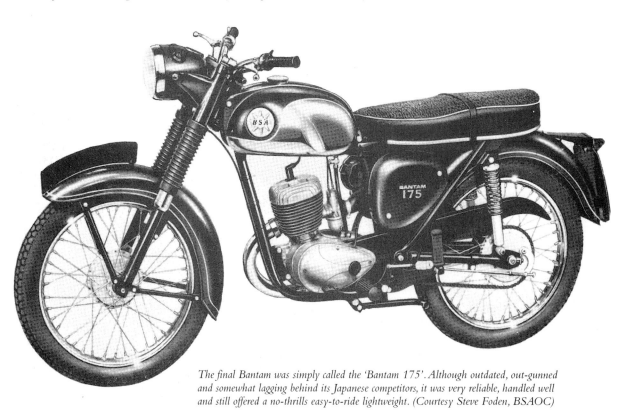

The final Bantam was simply called the 'Bantam 175'. Although outdated, out-gunned and somewhat lagging behind its Japanese competitors, it was very reliable, handled well and still offered a no-thrills easy-to-ride lightweight. (Courtesy Steve Foden, BSAOC)

Bantams and all other BSAs together for over a century. The Bantam home mechanic now had to buy a set of A/F spanners to fettle his new B175.

The most honest contemporary road test for the B175 came courtesy of *Meccano* magazine. In June 1970 it commended the Bantam for good overall value for money and high-quality finish, but lambasted its old-fashioned looks and lack of extras such as an integral steering head lock and a reserve fuel tap. For £134, the report thought it worthy of consideration. The bike would have scored more points if the speedometer had been illuminated (someone must have pinched the bulb) and if the steering locking system had actually been provided with a padlock.

The B175 was one of the outstanding 175s, with slightly better manners than the D14/4. The engine was solid and the superior handling put anything else to shame. Its only weakness lay in the electrical parts, as there was a tendency to over-charge the battery on long daylight runs. Perhaps it was a fitting tribute that the last Bantam should be one of the finest.

A BSA Bushman impressing the girls in Cameroon in 1970. It might have made a difference if the dip switch was connected! (Courtesy Peter Glover)

Resilient Bantam B175s and Bushmans were doing a roaring trade for Fako Automobile Company in Cameroon in 1970. They all probably still going strong! (Courtesy Peter Glover)

D10, D14/4 and B175 models

Engine details

Model series	D10	D14/4	B175
Year produced	1966–67	1968	1969–71
Capacity	174cc	174cc	174cc
Bore × stroke	61.5 × 58mm	61.5 × 58mm	61.5 × 58mm
Comp ratio	8.65:1	10.0:1	9.5:1
Claimed power	10bhp @ 6,000rpm	12.6bhp @ 5,750rpm	12.6bhp @ 5,750rpm
Carburation	Amal 626 concentric	Amal R626 concentric	Amal R626 concentric

Ignition and lighting

D10–B175: Wipac 60-watt alternator. Coil ignition. Battery lighting.
Some models with energy transfer ignition.

Transmission

		D10		D14/4		B175	
		3-speed	4-speed	Std	Bushman	Std	Bushman
Gear ratios	Fourth	N/A	6.57	6.58	8.1	6.58	8.1
	Third	6.57	8.55	8.55	10.5	8.55	10.5
	Second	9.25	12.03	12.04	14.8	12.04	14.8
	First	17.35	18.68	18.68	23.0	18.68	23.0
Clutch – friction plates				4		4	
Chains – primary							
Size		3/8in × 0.25in		3/8in × 0.25in		3/8in × 0.25in	
No pitches		50		50		50	
Rear							
Size		½in × 0.335in		½ × 0.335in		½ × 0.335in	
No pitches		120		120 (128 B'man)		121 (128 B'man)	
No sprocket teeth							
Engine		17		17		17	
Gearbox		16		16		16	
Clutch Chainwheel		38		38		38	
Rear Chainwheel		46 (58 B'man)		47 (58 B'man)		47 (58 B'man)	

Suspension

	D10	D14/4	B175
Front	Teles. coil spring, hydraulically damped	Teles. coil spring, hydraulically damped	Teles. coil spring, hydraulically damped
Rear	Swing-arm. Girling spring-hyd units	Swing-arm. Girling spring-hyd units	Swing-arm. Girling spring-hyd units

Capacities	D10	D14/4	B175
Fuel tank			
Imp gallons	1 7/8	1 7/8	1 7/8
Petroil mixture			
Ratio	20:1	24:1 (4%)	24:1 (4%)
Gearbox	¾ pint	¾ pint	¾ pint

Wheels			
Brake size			
Dia	5½in	5½in	5½in
Width	1in	1in	1in
Rim size			
Front	WM1–18	WM1–18	WM1–18
Rear	WM1–18 (WM2-19 B'man)	WM1–18	WM1–18
Tyre size			
Front	3.00–18	3.00–18	3.00–18
Rear	3.00–18	3.00–18	3.00–18

Dimensions			
Seat height	30½in (762.5mm)	30½in (762.5mm)	30½in (762.5mm)
Wheelbase	50in (1250mm)	50in (1250mm)	50in (1250mm)
Weight (inc 1 gallon of petroil)	226lb (102.75kg)	225lb (102.25kg)	225lb (102.25kg)

Performance (extracted from published road test data)			
Top speed	64mph (102.5km/h)	64mph (102.5km/h)	62mph (99km/h)
Acceleration	Standing quarter-mile in 22 secs	Standing quarter-mile in 22 secs	Standing quarter-mile in 22 secs
Braking distance from 30mph to rest.	32ft	29ft 6in	30ft
Fuel consumption	130mpg @ 40mph (2.17ltr/100km @ 65km/h), 118mpg @ 50mph (2.4ltr/100km @ 80km/h)	105mpg @ 40mph (2.7ltr/100km @ 65km/h), 85mpg @ 50mph (3.33ltr/100km @ 80km/h)	110mpg @ 40mph (2.55ltr/100km @ 65km/h), 90mpg @ 50mph (3.15ltr/100km @ 80km/h)

The Demise of the Bantam

Of the 56,200 motorcycles exported from Britain in 1970, the vast majority were supplied by BSA-Triumph. It seemed as if the management had been shaken out of their complacency and a brighter, more secure future was assured. In February 1967, BSA Managing Director Lionel Jofeh, one of many high-flying executives brought in from the aircraft industry, instigated a new research and development establishment division at Umberslade Hall in Hockley Heath, Warwickshire. However, the running costs amounted to £1 million and,

The last days of Bantam production. Small Heath General Works Manager Alistair Cave explains the situation to the incumbent BSA Managing Director Lionel Jofeh. (Courtesy Alistair Cave)

although the number of ideas came thick and fast, the useful designs that came out of Umberslade Hall were few and far between. When the epoch-making 750cc three-cylinder Triumph Trident and BSA Rocket III models were announced, in autumn 1968, all attention was focused on the new 'Superbike' age. It would be BSA-Triumph's last stand. Within a few months, the 67bhp four-cylinder Honda CB750 appeared, with a five-speed gearbox, electric start and hydraulic disc brake, indicators and all mod cons.

BSA-Triumph fared little better in the medium-size market. A brave new 350cc OHC design should have been a winner but it was premature, badly made and soaked up a fortune in tooling costs. Major design faults were discovered and only a few prototypes ever saw the light of day.

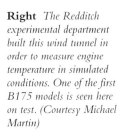

Above *Small Heath Works Manager Alistair Cave (left) shows newly appointed Managing Director Lionel Jofeh a skilled coach painter hand-lining a fuel tank. (Courtesy Alistair Cave)*

Right *The Redditch experimental department built this wind tunnel in order to measure engine temperature in simulated conditions. One of the first B175 models is seen here on test. (Courtesy Michael Martin)*

Above *The rare 1968 prototype D18 Bantam Trials with an alloy barrel. It was ridden by Mick Bowers in the Scottish Six Days Trial, coming in tenth. Umberslade Hall, BSA's research and development establishment, stands in the background. (Courtesy Michael Martin)*

Left *A close-up of the D18 alloy barrel prototype campaigned by Mick Bowers in 1968. (Courtesy Michael Martin)*

Interest in lightweights had not entirely gone, but the 50cc two-stroke, three-wheeled shopping basket, shamelessly named the Ariel 3, brought final calamity. Investment in tooling, materials and advertising had been massive, yet, within a few weeks of its launch, only a handful had been sold. It was a monumental blunder that cost BSA £2 million.

At the bottom of the pile lay the Bantam 175, which would be the first victim in the draconian measures that followed.

The Bantam development section was transferred to Umberslade Hall and the Redditch factory was closed for good in 1970. Only a handful of employees were willing to transfer to Small Heath, and the rest accepted redundancy packages. One of Michael Martin's last developments at Umberslade Hall was a promising revamp of the B175 with full-width hubs and modern 'upside-down' forks. An entirely new 200cc engine was also tried out in a scaled-down B25 frame, but it was not to be.

Trying to build too many models caused havoc with production, delivery and sales. In 1971, the company had 13 new or modified models listed. It ran into production difficulties, missed the important North American spring market and plunged £8.5 million into arrears. The remedy was as drastic as it was necessary. Under the guidance of Lord Shawcross, the model range was rationalized to concentrate solely on 650cc twins and 750cc triples. The 250 and 440cc Gold Star and Victor singles were dropped, as was the Bantam. It had gone through three engine sizes, five frames, four sets of forks and so many changes that only a handful of parts survived from the old rigid D1.

The B175 had been part of the much-publicized line-up for 1971, which was to be the key to BSA's future fortunes. In fact, by March 1971, the Bantam had been discontinued. A realistic offer was made to the BSA board of directors for the purchase of the design rights by a well-known Bantam enthusiast and race tuner, who saw the potential for the well-established two-stroke. Instead, the jigs and fixtures were unforgivably smashed to pieces with a sledgehammer, witnessed by journalist Bob Currie. After twen-ty-three years of cheap, safe and sensible transport for many thousands of owners and generations of learners, and half a million Bantams, it all ended.

After the Bantam

When news of the demise of the Bantam was announced, both press and public poured scorn on the decision. A sense of loss pervaded the motorcycling world. The Bantam, once the butt of a few jokes and the subject of silly tales of der-ring-do, was suddenly seen in a different light as an ever-safe and reliable runabout. The vacuum was filled by various machines produced in the former Soviet block countries. There were more than enough riders who could see through the built-in obsolescence of the Japanese motorcy-cles. Products from CZ and Jawa embodied all that had been found in BSA's runabout, earning themselves the nickname of 'Commy bloc Bantams'. The most popular was the MZ, which, in spite of Cold-War politics, has survived as the clear descendant and original survivor of the late 1930s DKW RT125.

After the war the DKW company re-established itself at Ingolstadt in the former West Germany and began to develop two-stroke racing motorcycles. The old Zschopauer Motorradwerk fell into the Russian sector and the factory was dismantled by the Red Army. However, in 1956 the company was rebuilt and went back into manufacture. The incumbent regime turned the factory's initials around to create a name – MZ (Motorrad Zschopau) – for a range of two-stroke motorcycles that became the longest-living descendants of the original 'Little Miracle'. Unlike most other East German industries, which were frozen in a late-1940s time warp, the MZ and its brilliant engineer Walter Kaarden extended the boundaries of two-stroke engine development. The company was soon producing up to 80,000 machines a year. By 1983, total output had passed two million.

In 1962, MZ's top-rate Grand Prix rider and technician, Ernst Degner, defected to the West, taking with him most of MZ's advanced technology. Japanese company Suzuki was just one of

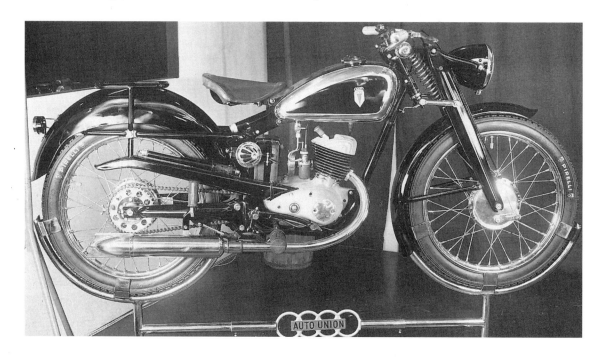

Above *A DKW RT125 on show during the early 1950s. The similarity to the BSA Bantam is clear. (Courtesy Mick Walker)*

Left *'Al Cave, This is Your Life.' In December 1982, Birmingham's best-loved boss retired having spent 41 years with BSA. On retirement he was Managing Director of Hale Engineering, a remnant of the old BSA empire then producing parts for Massey-Ferguson. With him on the pillion of a 1966 D7 Bantam Super is his wife Irene. Presenting the famous red book is John Balder, former Manufacturing Director of BSA. All those in attendance are ex-BSA employees. (Courtesy Alistair Cave)*

many that profited from this, transforming itself from a struggling textile machine manufacturer to one of the big four Japanese motorcycle makers. Their first motorcycle, the Colleda, was another from the template of the RT125.

The once-imposing BSA Small Heath factory, a Birmingham landmark on the corner of Armoury Road and the Golden Hillock Road, is long gone. In 1978, the bulldozers laid waste all its bricks and mortar. Today a part of the old site is occupied by supermarket chain Morrisons, and a large plaque commemorates the days of the Birmingham Small Arms company, the Gold Star and the other superb motorcycles that once carried the piled-arms motif. The factory on Studley Road, Redditch, where Bantam engines were built, was closed down by BSA in 1970. Parts of the building are still in existence today although the site is much less impressive than it used to be.

In 1998, Ken Ascott celebrated the 50th anniversary of the Bantam by riding from Land's End to John O'Groats on his 1956 D1. XJH 134 did the 874 miles (nearly 1400km) without any problems. (Courtesy Ken Ascott)

Estimates of total Bantam production have ranged widely, with most references talking of over half a million units. More recent totting up from despatch records points to just over 400,000 bikes built and shipped. In the scheme of modern automotive production, this was not a massive amount – the one-millionth Morris Minor car was built in 1961 and Standard-Triumph produced 700,000 Herald and Vitesse cars. The Bantam did hold the record for motorcycle production, but this has been soundly eclipsed by the Honda 'step-thru' Cub, which must account for over 10 million units, and rising. When BSA made anything, they never did things by half even if it was for a limited batch. They tooled up and the parts poured out. Huge amounts of Bantam spares were dispersed through the entire old dealer network and Bantam treasure troves are always being discovered.

Large stocks of ex-factory Bantam spares found their way on to the market, many of them acquired by Bob Joyner of Wolverhampton, who for many years satisfied a thriving mail order market. Cash-on-delivery spares would arrive at the customer's door wrapped in a Black Country newspaper like a portion of fish and chips. This holding has since been dispersed throughout the

Bantams went everywhere – in Papua New Guinea slight modifications to a missionary's bike were essential for fording a river. (Courtesy Alistair Cave)

A 1971 artist's impression of a proposed new-generation BSA Bantam. Alas, it was not to be. (Courtesy Michael Martin)

trade and Bantam owners will continue to be supported for many years to come.

From time to time rumours about reviving the BSA Bantam have often circulated. In 1976 following a management buy-out with the rights to call themselves 'The BSA Company', a range of lightweight bikes was designed for limited production using Yamaha and Morini engines. After moving premises to Blockley in Gloucestershire well over 1,000 machines bearing the BSA Bushman name had left the works for third world countries. At least the Bushman albeit with a Yamaha engine remains as popular as ever somewhere on the globe. After a round of moves and mergers, the now Southampton based BSA Regal company is staged to revive the BSA motorcycle with plans for an exciting large capacity twin to compliment their handsome hand-built 500cc Gold Star.

In recent times MZ was reorganized after German unification to become MuZ (Motorrad und Zweiradwerk). In collaboration with the British based Seymour-Powell design studio set out to bring back the Bantam name, feeling there was a thriving market for frugal get-to-work machine bike but attractively styled and an up to date specification. Although the company makes a successful range of Rotax engined Scorpion models, we still wait with bated breath for a new Bantam.

Despite whatever plans are made for the revival of the name it could never be the same as the original. After years of relative disinterest, Bantams are now being restored to former glory. The BSA Owners Club, The British Two-Stroke Club and the Vintage Motorcycle Club have seen their ranks swelled by people who have recovered a long lost and forgotten Bantam hoping to revive a little piece of old England. That Birmingham cockerel will continue to puff out its proud breast and crow.

5 Go Bantam Go!

The BSA Bantam was supposed to be a low-cost utility for getting people to work. When it first appeared in 1948 the very notion of using one for trials, scrambling or road racing would never have been taken seriously. Yet the basic design was the fruit of intensive experimentation in two-stroke engines by DKW before the Second World War. With the Schnuerle twin loop scavenging system, full circular flywheels and an integral gearbox, BSA had inherited a 125cc engine that was efficient, fundamentally correct and offered massive scope for improvement. The Bantam engine was used in every branch of motorsport, although much of its success was attributable to private builders and engine tuners.

Bantams and Motorsport

Weekend off-road observation trials provided clubman privateers with affordable motorsport. Many recognized the excellent power to weight ratio of the Bantam and home-brewed 'specials'

Left *BSA's competition expert Brian Martin tries out the prototype swing-arm frame 150cc Bantam Competition model on the Small Heath factory test track, probably in 1956. (Courtesy Steve Foden, BSAOC)*

Opposite *With stuffer plates in the crankcase, a skimmed-down cylinder head and a king-size rear sprocket, a Bantam can jump through hoops! This Bantam scrambler was based on a D7 model. (Courtesy Peter Glover)*

H.D. Rodgers were the BSA agents for Uganda in the 1960s. Here one of their mechanics, Mlikasa, performs tricks on a Bantam. Note the absence of a front brake! (Courtesy Alistair Cave)

began to participate. BSA was receptive to the demand and almost at once a Competition D1 model was offered with a larger rear sprocket, raised saddle and exhaust, and the lighting equipment removed.

The first BSA factory-supported rider to pick up a trophy was George Pickering, a former Army despatch rider turned BSA road tester, who won the 125cc class in the 1950 Colmore Cup. This was just the first in a long list of awards and wins for George Pickering and many other privately backed riders. Throughout the early 1950s Bantams recorded more wins in trials than all other makes put together. Even George Fisher, who would go on to win glory for the Coven-

try-built Francis-Barnett, began his career on a Bantam, winning the Beggar's Roost, Cotswold Cup and Wye Valley Traders Trophy in the process. In the high-status International Six Days Trial, the D1 Competition Bantam was beset with bad luck. George Pickering was on a clean sheet with just one day to go in the 1950 ISDT, but poor route-marking threw him off course and out of time.

When the 150cc D3 Major appeared with a swing-arm frame, the Bantam regained some of its competitive edge even though official 'over-the-counter' competition models had been discontinued. A prototype model ridden by John Draper won both the Mitcham Vase and the Manville Trial at the first time of asking but gradually the three-speed Bantam was being overtaken and outclassed by more developed machinery such as the DOT-Villiers. Victories in trials would still be won by Bantams, albeit infrequently, notably by D.H. Barrett in the 1957 150cc Welsh Trophy Trial and then by Ken Sedgley in the 1959 175cc class Victory Cup Trial. The high-water mark of the trials Bantam came in 1967 when Mick Bowers claimed the 200 class cup in the Cotswold and then Dave Rowland managed a second placing on a 175cc D10 in the prestigious Scottish Six Days Trial.

The Bantam also made an immediate impact when organized scrambles re-started after the war. Bill Nicholson was testing and developing the original prototype 123cc D1 Trials competition bike before they even thought of the name Bantam, and went on to win the 1950 Cotswold Scramble 125cc class on a re-geared version. This was followed by another dominant performance at Shrublands Park but, gradually, competition became more serious and outright victories harder to come by. Notable wins came in the 1956 and 1957 Experts Grand National meetings. Brian Stonebridge and John Draper both

came from the back of the field to steal a one-two for the BSA Bantam in the 1956 event, Draper winning by the thickness of a spoke.

Australian Racing – Eric Walsh

The potential for tuning a Bantam to make faster tracks was first recognized in Australia, where motorcycle racing had evolved from paddock racing dominated by big-bore OHV singles. Eric Walsh had been one of the pre-war stars on the rough tracks but, after sustaining a bad injury, he decided to concentrate on engine and racing development and turned his attention to the recently imported BSA Bantam. In 1950 he developed and created the first in a series of machines that won virtually all contested racing on road and dirt for six consecutive years. The most convincing wins were in the 1952 and 1954 Australian TT, when Maurie Quincey piloted the winning Walsh Bantam home. Also in 1952, Ken

Michael Martin winning the 150cc class in the Terry Cups Trial 1957. The machine is an ex-John Draper D3 Bantam Major with a Herman Meirer engine. Michael Martin went on to become responsible for Bantam development at Redditch. His brother, the late Brian Martin, was BSA Competitions Manager from 1960. (Courtesy Michael Martin)

Above *'G'day sport!'*
Australian Bantam speed
pioneers established nine
Australian 125cc class
records at Sellicks Beach,
South Australia, in March
1950. The riders are Don
Dixon, Bruce Hector and
Frank Johns. (Courtesy
Mick Walker)

Left *The all-conquering*
Walsh Bantam in
full flight, piloted by
H. Rumble during a race
at Fisherman's Bend in
around 1954. The bike
could achieve over 100mph
(160km/h) on an open
megaphone exhaust.
(Courtesy Steve Foden,
BSAOC)

Rumble won the Victoria 500cc scramble title on a Walsh-tuned Bantam, seeing off a complete field of 500cc big bangers and some of the latest twin OHC machines. In 1956 two works riders signed to Moto Guzzi visited Australia and were invited to a session on a Walsh alcohol-burning Bantam. Bill Lomas and Dickie Dale each cracked the 100mph barrier on a number of occasions. The Walsh Bantam they rode was reckoned to be the fastest 125cc-powered machine in the world.

In 1957 Walsh decided to get his name in the Aussie speed record books with a completely streamlined 125cc Bantam. The cigar-shaped all-enclosed Bantam managed 115mph before ignition troubles curtailed any further attempts.

Sadly, Eric Walsh died some years ago. Virtually unknown in the UK, he was once a national hero in Australia, ranking alongside cricketer Don Bradman in renown. Walsh was a pioneer of the racing two-stroke engine and had given the Bantam, otherwise seen by the racing fraternity as a cheap runabout for learners and old ladies, its own reverence and respect.

After Walsh, other Australian rider/mechanics picked up where he left off. The Hogan brothers appeared in the weekend round-up of sports results with regularity, and their 'high-torque' cylinder head design became a much sought-after accessory. They operated from Warren Garage in Pinner Green, Middlesex, and offered a complete go-faster kit that added at least 5mph to any Bantam.

Much of the success of the early Australian pioneers was achieved long before anyone understood the merits of harnessing exhaust back pressure and controlled expansion chambers. The Walsh Bantams achieved high engine speeds and blistering performance on nothing more than an open exhaust feeding through a large megaphone silencer!

An amazing, fully streamlined Walsh Bantam makes an attack on the 125cc speed record in 1957. It reached a top speed of 115mph (185km/h). (Courtesy Mortons Motorcycle Media)

Left *H. Rumble on a Walsh Bantam heads for yet another victory. (Courtesy Steve Foden, BSAOC)*

Below *An Eric Walsh Bantam ridden by H. Rumble on its way to another Australian win, this time on grass. (Courtesy Steve Foden, BSAOC)*

The 1954 Patras to Athens race for two-strokes was won by Nicholas Papaoutsas on a 150cc D3 Bantam Major. He covered the 135 miles (220km) in 3 hours and 16 minutes. (Courtesy Alistair Cave)

Racing in Britain

In Britain, the Bantam had its champion in George Todd, who, like the Hogan brothers, produced a range of go-faster kits and after-sales accessories. One of these was the Todd GT cylinder head, which could stand 15 tons per square inch pressure at a constant 300 degrees centigrade, and enabled a compression ratio of 12.5:1. Todd spent countless hours of working and experimenting with port shapes and various engine modifications, but he was willing to share his hard-won expertise. In 1956 he published

Boost up your Bantam, a set of notes and explanations for anyone wishing to make their little cockerel really fly.

Todd, a proven rider at the controls of a racing Bantam, also built and tuned engines for others. The most outstanding racer using a Todd Bantam, and an ex-GPO one at that, was Fred Launchbury. In the 1967 125cc Isle of Man TT he came in 20th, at an average speed of 73.96mph (118.33km/h). Launchbury had a business in Raynes Park, London, trading formula Bantam racing equipment. When fairings were eventually allowed by the Bantam Racing Club, the

Neil Andrew in action during a Formula Bantam season. (Courtesy Neil Andrew)

Racing for beginners. Neil Andrew started his Bantam racing career in the late 1960s with a worn-out D1 and a little help from his Pal 'DK'. He practised on an old airfield near Desborough, Northamptonshire, and went on to collect twenty-five trophies and forty-six placings in Formula Bantam. (Courtesy Neil Andrew)

Launchbury fairing was outstanding. It was a sad day for all when Fred was killed whilst racing a 250cc Maico on the Isle of Man in 1979.

Race-tuned Bantams became so popular that entire meetings were organized for them. In 1960, a group of enthusiasts, mainly from the Wimbledon MCC and led by Bunny Armstrong, formulated what eventually became the Bantam Racing Club. The rules were straightforward: all racers were to retain the original diamond frame and crankcases; engines were limited to 125cc and three gears only. After that it was anything goes. In the early days some racers carried on using the original Wico-Pacy ignition and non-damped Bantam forks, and the accepted improvement in the braking department was to weld two front hubs back to back. It may have been racing on the cheap but guile, ingenuity and innovation led to rapid progress. Modern forks, swing-arm suspension and electronic beam-triggered ignition arrived. Various crankshaft components from Japanese engines were fitted inside the Bantam cases to provide short-stroke high-revving engines; even water-cooling was used to good effect!

The BRC lap speed record at Snetterton started at 65mph (105km/h) and soon went up to 81mph (130km/h). In 1972, Mick 'Sticky' Scutt averaged 74mph (118km/h) around the Isle of Man TT course in appalling weather. Tony Jones finished a commendable 8th in 1974 with a best lap of 26 minutes, 44 seconds.

The Bantam Racing Club was a democratic

Neil Andrew gets his head down as the Bantam goes on to full chime. The lower half of the fairing was damaged in an earlier spill, giving up a few secrets in exhaust design! (Courtesy Neil Andrew)

organization and changes to the rules were only invoked by popular vote at an AGM. Alloy rims and non-steel fuel tanks were eventually allowed and when the club produced a tuning guide for novices it was reasonable for a newcomer to raise 8,000rpm out of an old rooster, polished, ported, fettled and packed with compression plates.

Thousands of people learnt to ride on a Bantam, and the BRC was the starting point for many a blossoming career. Roy Bacon was one successful rider in the early years who, along with Fred Launchbury, George Todd, Bob Newby Mick Scutt and Tony Jones, was entered into the International Isle of Man TT races by the BRC. Roy Bacon did his stint as Chairman of the BRC between 1964-69 before becoming an acclaimed writer and motorsports journalist. Formula 1 Racing World Champion Damon Hill and twice 500cc World Champion Barry Sheene both once raced a Bantam. Even Mick Grant, somewhere in the middle of his career, did a turn on a Bantam because the bike he was 'booked' to ride did not

show up! Other well-known riders who started out on Bantams were motorcross champion Graham Noyce and Neil Tuxworth, who had a fantastic TT career and then went on to manage Castrol Honda UK Racing.

Aside from the renowned stars there were other heroes who, were it not for the affordable access to Bantam racing, would not have been able to endure in motorsports. One who rose quickly through the ranks was Peter Styles of Ilford, Essex. After watching some lightweight class racing he decided to take part, and he went on to win the BRC championship for three consecutive years, from 1979 to 1981.

Home Improvements

Bantam tuning was not only targeted at racing; a few simple modifications, that were well within the realms of a home mechanic, could vastly improve the running efficiency of an ordinary road-going bike. George Todd advised on three

levels of tuning methods to suit all needs: simple, intermediate and advanced. Simple tuning amounted to improving fits and accuracy, and close examination of the engine bearings. The effects could be dramatic. Todd recognized from the start that improved running accuracy gave improved performance so the crankshaft would be checked to ensure there was no measurable or down movement in the main bearings and crank-end float was kept within .005'. The oilite bush fitted in the end of the stator for instance was

Opposite Ted Hodgson Jnr, son of US BSA President Theodore Hodgson, takes the chequered flag (literally) after winning two events in one afternoon on a 150cc Bantam. Perhaps a piece of tablecloth was all they could find! (Courtesy Steve Foden, BSAOC)

Below On an open megaphone, John Kirkby running wild at Cadwell Park, 1964. Still with Bantam forks and plunger rear end but a 'hi-torque' cylinder head gives it some edge. (Courtesy Mick Walker)

often the most neglected part in the engine and yet it was crucial to both precision and performance. A worn stator bush caused excessive crankshaft whip and therefore had a detrimental effect on main bearing life and performance. To get the best out of any engine, the bush had to be in tip-top condition.

The condition of the cylinder was also vital for any amount of improvement. The standard piston clearances were given as .012in at the crown and .006in at the skirt. If wear was greater than .005in the cylinder would need a re-bore in which case it was recommended to hone the bore .001in oversize and fit a chrome piston ring in the top groove. The first few hundred miles of careful running-in were also crucial to any Bantam whether new from a showroom or fettled for the racetrack.

For racing, big-end bearing up and down movement was only tolerated up to .003in and no appreciable movement should be present

between the gudgeon pin and small-end bush. Cleanliness and polishing of the engine internals, especially the inlet and exhaust ports and the transfer tracts, also made a useful contribution to performance. The idea was to improve gas flow and reduce primary fuel charge turbulence.

To raise the compression ratio the shoulders on the cylinder head could be machined completely away, provided the 52mm hemispherical combustion space was not reduced. This increased the compression ratio to 8.3:1 and, to reduce any risk of pre-ignition, the radius around the edge of the spark plug recess could be round-

H. Rumble gets both wheels off the ground during a hectic scramble held at Port Henry, Australia, in 1954. (Courtesy Steve Foden, BSAOC)

ed, to remove any hot spots. The alternative was to fit a Hogan 'high-torque' cylinder head. For higher compressions, the ignition timing would be retarded for points opening at 22 degrees BTDC or 7/64in if measuring the piston position. This would involve extending the slots in the stator plate fixing lugs. The carburettor would also require re-jetting and this could only be resolved through trial and error. Anything from a size 110 to an 85 main jet would have to be tried to gain the best results. The objective was to get the plug electrode showing a dark brown colour after a good burst of full throttle. The effect of running high revs on a raised compression invariably demanded a cool running spark plug. Finally, the pre-1954 'flat-Bantam' silencer might have looked pretty on the basic D1 but gave too much back pressure on a performance bike so the later

The BANTAM CROWED AT CATALINA!!

After a tortuous 50-mile (80-km) mountain road race in 1952, seven of the twenty-eight entrants were on BSA Bantams and all seven finished, four of them in the top five placings. The winner was Ray Weimen on his 'Snarlin Darlin' BSA Bantam. (Courtesy Steve Foden, BSAOC)

long tubular silencer with detachable baffles became a definite must-have.

With such simple modifications an otherwise standard Bantam would certainly start to move more briskly. For a sportier performance, the breathing of the engine had to be improved. This next stage of intermediate tuning work required a small pistol drill with flexible drive and assorted rotary files to re-profile the ports. This became a specialized art form and numerous port and piston skirt cut-away combinations were evolved for both pre-54 'pineapple' and post-54 later large-fin cylinders. The object was to alter the port timing to give increased openings. It was no straightforward matter of making the ports as large as possible; the importance of the relationships with piston position, skirt shape, exhaust characteristics and carburation turned the matter into an exact science. The standard carburettor air filter had to bee thrown away and a new intake tube or trumpet made up. A tube length of 1?in (31.25mm) from the spigot recess to the bell-end flared out to 2in (50mm) diameter would normally suffice.

The achievement of any more power required more advanced methods of tuning, the resources of a machine shop and welding facilities. Padding plates fixed to the crankcase walls increased crankcase pressure and an alternative ignition system had to be used, usually involving a coil, capacitor or, later on, a light beam-triggered electronic set-up. Again, carburation was the key, so the old clip-fitting type had to be dispensed with by cutting away the barrel spigot, opening up the inlet tract to 7/8in and bronze-welding a flange to take a 275-type body. In this way, it was possi-

ble to attain 10,000rpm. The oil flow to the main bearings given by the existing petroil lubrication system would prove inadequate. Enlarging the feed ducts located just inside the crankcase mouth brought some improvement but the preferred route to better lubrication in a high-performance engine was to add an auxiliary pump and directly feed oil through 1/16in bore piping to the bearings. A single-stage Pilgrim pump could be fixed inside the primary drive case and driven from the clutch drum.

Gearing played an important part. With the extra power, the first step was to replace the standard 15-tooth gearbox sprocket for a 14-tooth. To clear the drive chain a special gearbox oil seal housing had to be fitted. The alternative gearbox

internals made available by the official D1 Competition Bantam, along with a 16-tooth gearbox sprocket, gave racers, scramblers and trials riders a choice of up to 24 different ratios, based on a standard 47-tooth rear-wheel sprocket. Many circuit racers used a gear cluster supplied by Snell engineering that lifted the first ratio.

Despite the monumental strides in racing development carried out by amateurs over many years, the BSA factory showed little interest. Indeed, it took some persistent arm-twisting and diplomacy before they agreed to supply a batch of close-ratio gears in 1967. Most of the requests of the trialists, scramblers and privateer road racers may have fell on deaf ears at Small Heath, but they ensured none the less that the humble Bantam had earned its place in motorsports history.

The BRC is still active and Formula Bantam racing continues to thrive, although it is now controlled under the wing of the Vintage MCC racing section. There is a full schedule of planned meetings and it remains the easiest way for anyone to start racing.

Opposite *The start of the 1954 Monsoon Rally in Ceylon. This 125cc D1 Bantam had been entered by local BSA distributor Cargills. (Courtesy Steve Foden, BSAOC)*

Below *This Formula Bantam racer was prepared and raced by John Danks. (Courtesy Alistair Cave)*

Meticulous preparation for a Formula Bantam racer at Mallory Park, 2002. (Owen Wright)

Bantam Racing Days

In 1966, Mick Barr watched a 125cc race at Snetterton race circuit in Norfolk, and was awestruck by the sight of a BSA Bantam lapping at over 70mph (110km/h). He was hooked. He sold his Gold Star, bought a van and a copy of *Tuning for Speed*, and set about building a Formula Bantam racer. At the time, he was working as a mechanic for Jack Gunnell, a motorcycle dealership on Welford Road, Leicester. Gunnell held the BSA agency so there were plenty of Bantams around, and a limitless supply of 'free' spares. The only money Barr had to spend was on a set of close-ratio gears from Snell Engineering.

'The gearbox conversion consisted of just two gears, which raised the first gear ratio. It cost 12 shillings and 8 pence,' recalls Barr. 'In the following year Jack Gunnell managed to get one of the limited-issue Bantam close-ratio gear sets for me direct from BSA, and I had to hand over £12 – a full week's wages!'

The new ratios made all the difference. In March 1967, Mick Barr entered his first race at Snetterton. With forty starters in two races he managed to come in twelfth and ninth – not bad for a first day out. Taking a look at the quicker bikes, he noticed that most were using D7 forks and brakes, strengthened frames, Girling shock absorbers, coil ignition and a rev counter run off the mainshaft via a modified primary chaincase cover. Despite using the original Wipac flywheel magneto and D1 forks, the first Mick Barr Bantam was still managing 68mph (108km/h) down the long straight.

The biggest obstacle to any gain in performance was crankcase sealing. Barr's engine was yet another victim of the dreaded screwdriver-lever-between-the-crankcases. In 1968, he took a job as a vehicle mechanic for Leicestershire police. One day the Underwater Search Unit found a complete Bantam 150cc D3 in the canal and asked if he wanted any of the remains. It was clear that the engine had never been taken apart and therefore offered a better prospect for tuning. The later 150cc 'big sleeve' motor was much stronger and less liable to distortion as the temperature rose. The same cylinder was ported with an extra transfer port just above the inlet. A specially machined cast-iron sleeve with exactly the same size ports was pressed in and bored out to 125cc. After further blending and polishing of the ports, an Omega piston carrying just one ring was fitted. To take the expected power increase a D14/4 clutch with

stronger springs replaced the tired-out D1 unit and a 30mm Amal carburettor was mounted on to a brazed flange. The result was one of the most reliable and quickest Bantam racers ever.

Mick Barr won a cabinet full of trophies: 'Over 65 awards won, the best was winning the 1978 50-mile [80-km] 26-lap enduro at Snetts at the third attempt. It made up for the previous year when a failed big end stopped me whilst I was leading.'

Improvements were constantly being made. Alpha Bearings of Dudley made con-rod assemblies for the Bantam Racing Club and these were a popular fitment. The flywheel mag was discarded, a very short mainshaft was fitted and a flat surface machined to take a Motoplat ignition kit. In 1968, the BRC allowed alloy wheel rims and any make of forks and brakes on the grounds of safety.

'After I made all the improvements I could see 9,750rpm pushing a 15 x 46 gearing although in the wet I would put a 47T sprocket on the rear hub but keep quiet about it,' says Barr. 'Close rivals would check my

Mick Barr in action at Mallory Park 1967 before fairings were allowed. The bike was a sleeved-down 150cc D3 that had been salvaged from the canal by the Underwater Search Unit of the Leicestershire Police. The engine had never been dismantled and therefore had no screwdriver lever marks, making it ideal for racing. Mick Barr went on to claim 65 awards. (Courtesy Mick Barr)

bike out and ask what gearing I was pushing. I'd then change the sprocket at the last moment before a wet race! Also I would often use a tinted visor so as not to see any puddles laying on the track. What you can't see, you don't worry about, it worked for me, and I always did very well in the wet.'

The cost of Bantam racing worked out at £8 for three rides including rider insurance, and £10 for fuel, van and BSA. The finance was raised by repairing the private cars of Leicestershire's police officers!

continued overleaf

continued from page 147

In time several riders began to build short-stroke engines. Mick Barr followed suit by machining new flywheels to take a Yamaha TZ 250 con-rod assembly and piston. The cylinder was also machined to take a jacket for water-cooling. A special alloy cylinder head was cast at a college night school and some of the 'new' parts were taken from scrapped vehicles collected at the police garage.

In 1979, Jack Gunnell retired from business and his BSA shop came up for sale. Mick Barr's wife Glenyse struck a deal with Gunnell and the business was soon renamed 'Mick Barr Motorcycle Services', offering repairs of Bantams as well as other BSA, Norton and BMW machinery.

'We sold a lot of Bantam bits, new and used as there was still a large number of Bantam owners about,' says Mick Barr. 'One owner with a tatty well-used Bantam came in to buy main bearings and seals, and showed me photos of a trip he had made to Poland where he had had to change the mains at the side of the road!'

After leaving the shop on Welford Road, Mick Barr had a busy time working as an independent BMW specialist, using his experience from his police days. But there was to be another chapter in the Mick Barr Bantam story.

Patrol motorcyclist PC Clive Dawkes, attached to Leicester Central Traffic Division, had always fancied having a go at racing but lacked the financial and technical support. Mick Barr, then working as a transport unit mechanic, offered him a ride on his racing Bantam. 'Mick had recently retired from competitive racing and asked me if I was interested in riding his 1954 125cc Bantam in club competition. The chance was too good to miss,' explains Dawkes. The Barr-Dawkes racing team made its debut at Snetterton on 5 March 1977, but it was an inauspicious start. Clive Dawkes fell off during practice, when the engine seized. The bike was soon put right and, undaunted, he was able to line up with thirty other entrants. The result was a win, first time out. The pair decided to enter the Intermediate race later in the day. Still wearing his orange novice's jacket on an outdated machine, Dawkes led from the start and completed a second sensational win. His progress in one day was more than most could hope to achieve in two years.

One month later the team took on the very best Formula Bantam racers at Cadwell Park. Against the best riders and the most advanced machines, Clive Dawkes still claimed a third placing. The season continued with a string of good results, including one first, two seconds and two thirds – and an eventual seventh place in the championship.

Clive Dawkes attacks Devil's Elbow during a Formula Bantam race at Mallory Park, 1978. (Courtesy Mick Barr)

6 So Help Me George!

The Wico-Pacy electrics – the heart and Achilles heel of the BSA Bantam

Problem Solving

At one time or another Bantam owners would be sure to encounter 'George' the Wipac man. If the flywheel generator was not working, George would come to the rescue and explain why.

Most owners could manage to adjust the points and play around with the ignition timing with a bit of trial and error. Some found that closing down the spark plug gap also helped but this was a cheap-skate, short-term remedy to overcome the fact that the generator, the contraption that was supposed to make electricity, was sick. Further meddling, poking and fiddling with the wires only made matters worse. Anyone who attempted to take the flywheel off without the correct extractor tool would get into the most horrendous mess. The sensible thing was to get the bike looked at by the nearest BSA dealer, who would then summon the help of the Wico-Pacy servicing manual, and George.

George was a fictional old sage who appeared in Wico-Pacy Corporation sales adverts and technical bulletins. He was a sort of father figure in a white technician's coat who cropped up in motorbike magazines advising on some of the technical problems of motorcycle electrical equipment. For those who had a BSA Bantam or any other bike fitted with a Wipac flywheel

George says….

magneto, George's snippets of technical wisdom were invaluable. George used to say that 90 per cent of all troubles were electrical. 'Always check the easy and obvious things first,' he would say, wisely. 'Never fiddle with the timing or the carburettor, look at the spark plug first and then the points.'

Plug whiskering was an accepted part of the ritual of riding a Bantam. Some suffered inces-

The Wipac logo. The company abbreviated its name from Wico-Pacy in the early 1960s.

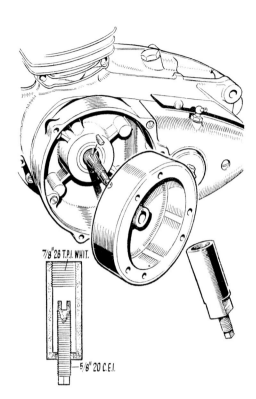

7/8" 26 T.P.I. WHIT.

—5/8" 20 C.E.I.

Removal of the flywheel should only be performed with the aid of the correct extractor tool.

santly, while others ran up massive mileages on the same plug. A sudden hesitancy, loss of power and then misfiring announced imminent plug fouling. Close inspection would reveal a tiny hair-like strand that straddled the electrode and plug body. A sharp puff of breath or the use of a thumbnail would make the plug serviceable once more. The whiskering depended upon riding conditions, oil, temperature or on the plug itself. Many riders persisted in carrying around a bag of worn-out plugs, but there was only one place for a second-hand spark plug – in the bin!

Wico-Pacy

Lucas electrical equipment was the mainstay fitting for a vast range of motorcycles from BSA, Triumph, Norton, Ariel and countless others – some of the directors at BSA held shares in Joseph Lucas Ltd so it was no surprise that the majority of contracts to supply the required mountains of magnetos and dynamos were placed with that company.

The Wico-Pacy Corp (later Wipac) was based in Buckingham, well outside the main Birmingham sphere of motorcycle manufacture. It survived therefore on selling small-batch, low-cost equipment, pared down to the barest necessity. Wipac switches in particular had a reputation for flimsiness, but, despite a number of shortcomings, in many cases Wipac electrics were fitted and forgotten. Many Bantamites even circumnavigated the world in blissful ignorance. In contrast, the Lucas 1A45 generators fitted to early 1950s De-Luxe Bantams were over-complicated and over-engineered.

Within five years of its launch, in 1948, an amazing 120,000 BSA D1 Bantams had been sold. The huge demand for generators, lamps and wiring harnesses constituted two-thirds of Wico-Pacy's factory output. Indeed, its neat and compact design of flywheel magneto generator certainly contributed to the success of the Bantam. Apart from a contract for 5,000 Lucas-supplied generators in 1950, all other Bantam models were Wipac-equipped, using any variation of the

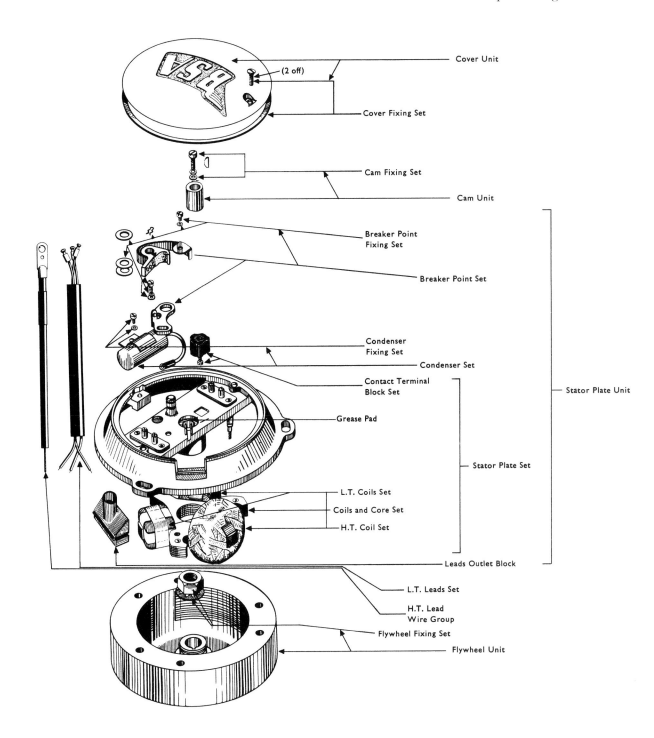

Cover Unit

(2 off)

Cover Fixing Set

Cam Fixing Set

Cam Unit

Breaker Point
Fixing Set

Breaker Point Set

Condenser
Fixing Set

Condenser Set

Contact Terminal
Block Set

Grease Pad

Stator Plate Unit

Stator Plate Set

L.T. Coils Set

Coils and Core Set

H.T. Coil Set

Leads Outlet Block

L.T. Leads Set

H.T. Lead
Wire Group

Flywheel Fixing Set

Flywheel Unit

Details of the Series 55 Mk 8 flywheel magneto generator, supplied in various forms and fitted to thousands of BSA Bantams.

Series 55 Mk 8 generator, until 1966, when the new D10 Bantam changed over to a true alternator and coil ignition system, again supplied by Wipac.

The Equipment

The Wico-Pacy flywheel magneto generator was an alternator and magneto rolled into one. It consisted of two main parts: a permanent magnet flywheel and a stator plate. The flywheel carried a number of laminated-iron permanent magnets moulded into a die-cast body and was keyed and locked on to the crankshaft.

The stator was also a die-cast component, located within a flywheel housing and clamped into place with three screws. Slotted holes in the stator plate enabled the assembly to be rotated for easy timing adjustment. The stator plate assembly carried a laminated iron core with projections or 'salient' poles to hold an ignition coil and various combinations of lighting coils. These were held in close proximity within the flywheel so that the orbiting magnets excited the coils and induced an alternating current (AC) to flow from each coil. (AC is an electrical current whose direction is regularly reversed.)

The larger coil, sitting on the uppermost pole, provided ignition. It actually consisted of two coils wrapped up in a shellac-coated bandage. Once again the wonders of electro-magnets, excited coils and the build-up of many thousands of volts aided and abetted by a contact breaker set provided a bright blue spark at the plug just when it was required…well, nearly.

The coils that fed into the lighting circuit occupied the lower stator poles and were wound from coarse-gauge copper wire. Depending on

Flywheel Magnetos		
Generator type	**Lighting output**	**Model details**
Geni-Mag	AC 6-volt 27-watt	D1 Bantams 1948 to 1951 up to engine YD1-40660.
IG.1130 (AC)	AC 6-volt 30-watt	Bantams up to August 1955. Replaced by IG.1452.
IG.1130 (DC)	DC 6-volt	Bantams up to August 1955. Replaced by IG.1450.
IG.1450	DC 6-volt	All Bantams with full DC lighting to May 1966.
IG.1452	AC 6-volt 30-watt	All Bantams with AC lighting (no battery or rectifier fitted).
IG.1552	AC 6-volt 30-watt, trickle charge.	Model D7 Super to Sept 63 (one switch in headlamp).
IG.1704	AC lights, trickle charge and coil ignition.	Model D7 Super from Oct 1963 to May 1966 (two switches in headlamp).

Alternators		
Generator type	**Lighting output**	**Model details**
GA1769	Full 6-volt DC coil ignition and lights.	D10, D14 Silver and Supreme. July 1966–Feb 1969.
GA1772	Full DC lights & ignition.	D10, D14 Sports and Bushman. Sept 1966–Feb 1969.
GA1776	Energy transfer ignition and AC lights.	D10, D14 Bushman. April 1967–Feb 1969.
GA1804	Full 6-volt DC coil ignition and lights.	Bantam 175 1969 on.
GA1806	Energy transfer ignition and AC lights.	Bushman 175 1969 on.

the type of generator, there were either two or three lighting coils. The alternating current (AC) flowing from the lighting coils could either run 'direct' to the lamps via a lighting switch in the headlamp shell, or could be converted to direct current (DC) by a rectifier to supply a more stabilized output into the lamp load and send a trickle charge to a battery. George was always having to explain the double meaning of the term 'direct' in the electrical context.

The rectifier was an especially sensitive and erratic component that was either a forgotten item that did a regular job for years, or an accursed affliction. On older machines it was circular, about 4in (100mm) in diameter, bolted to the rear mudguard below the saddle. It consisted of a series of plates that contained a substance called selenium, the electrical conductivity of which allowed the passage of current in one direction only. The old-type rectifiers relied on a good earth connection through the central mounting bolt. They were delicate items, hated vibration and were irreparably damaged if connected the wrong way. They also failed with age; by now there must be very few battery-lighting Bantams with their original rectifier intact. A modern replacement is a very small solid-state component that consists of a series of diodes connected in a bridge pattern and set within a resin.

Maintenance and Tuning

For engine strip-downs, a flywheel extractor tool was essential. The extractor was the only safe way of prising the heavy magnet flywheel from the crankshaft taper using a 7/8in 26 tpi 60-degree thread provided in the flywheel boss. Many a flywheel was irreparably damaged by a bout of hammering, levering or blasting with a blow torch!

Once the outer dished cover plate had been removed, the stator plate assembly exposed the contact breaker points and condenser set; the points were operated by a single lobe cam sitting on the end of the crankshaft.

Under normal use, only periodic checking of the points gap was required: the correct setting was .015in (marked on the stator body). George suggested a points check every 5,000 miles (8,000km), when it was also a good idea to polish the contact pads with a slither of wet or dry carborundum paper and apply a couple of drops of oil to the lubrication wick, without getting any on the points.

Starting troubles would invariably be traced to the spark plug, points or the timing position of the stator plate. Some problems were difficult to locate. For instance, the contact point pivot post on the stator plate could work loose and defy all efforts to get the machine to start or run; usually, one could be achieved, but not both. Individual owners developed all sorts of superstitions related to getting the motor fired up within half a dozen attempts: on Wednesdays, don't open the air strangler; don't flood the carb at any time after 9 o'clock; and if the moon is in Sagittarius, leave the bike at home and take the bus instead.

Removing a screw in the middle of the cam enabled the cam to be drawn from the crankshaft with a pair of point-nosed pliers Within the cam lurked a minute woodruff key, responsible for numerous timing problems. Due to variances in manufacturing tolerances, some owners found that the engine would not run unless the points were closed down to around .006in fully open. If both the flywheel and points cam woodruff keys were leaning in opposite directions, the points could open up before any decent voltage had been built up in the ignition coil. Closing the points gap down effectively retarded the ignition. One answer was to reverse the cam woodruff key. In case that failed, Wipac supplied a special cam, which opened the points 5 degrees late. It was the last resort.

The self-lubricating oilite bush in the middle of the stator plate prevented crankshaft whip and a resulting variance of timing or spark scatter. It was rarely necessary to replace it, but if this did need to be done, it was a difficult task. The worn bush had to be carefully removed by filing before pressing home a replacement. This then needed reaming out to suit the crank journal, giving around 0.0015in clearance, using a lathe and

Accessibility to the points on the Wipac Series 55 Mk 8 generators was very good. Note the felt wick lubricating the points cam. (Owen Wright)

locating from the stator body spigot to ensure exact concentricity.

Overheated coils could be identified by the tell-tale signs of burning and charring. Replacement coils were sold as a complete set and were fairly easy to fit provided a note had been made as to which wire went where. Wipac offered an exchange facility called the B4 service. The men behind the service counter never got used to the constant taunting: 'How long will it last "B4" I need a new one?' 'Does that mean it will pack up "B4" I get home?'

The condenser prevented arcing at the contact breaker pads. The condenser was connected across the points from low-tension (LT) lead to earth (stator body). Current cannot pass through a condenser because it consists of two metallic parts separated by an insulation medium (a dielectric). It acts as an energy reservoir for electrical energy that would otherwise burn away the points every time they were opened. The same condenser, Wipac number S1231, was fitted to all generators. Its rating is given as .25uF (micro-Farad). If a strong blue spark was emitted from the points when the engine was running, suspicion fell on a faulty condenser.

Variants and Spec Numbers

Wipac generators are still quite plentiful at auto-jumbles, but you will need to be able to recognize the various types and specification numbers. If there is a suffix B in the engine serial number stamped on the Bantam crankcase, battery lighting was fitted. The spec numbers for the Series 55 Mk 8 generators were usually engraved on the outer lip of the stator body.

The first Bantams were equipped with a device known as the Wico-Pacy 27-watt Geni-mag. The Geni-mag was a pure AC unit, providing alternating current straight to the head and tail lamps. The low wattage of these three-magnet flywheel generators was enough to ensure that the lamps would not be seriously overloaded at the maximum 6,000 to 7,000rpm engine speed. The ignition high-tension voltage could reach 8,000 volts at a 500rpm tick-over speed, climbing up to 14,000 volts at maximum revs. It was just enough to spark a model D1 into life.

The Geni-mag was really intended for ultra-lightweight cyclemotors and autocycles, and Wipac soon replaced it with something more robust. From August 1950, and Bantam engine number YD1 40661, the Geni-mag was replaced by a Series 55 Mk 8 generator to specification type IG1130. This was an AC/DC unit and could utilize a full-wave rectifier in the wiring harness to feed a trickle charge to a 6-volt battery and provide a stabilized DC output for lighting and an electric horn. AC Bantams had a rubber bulb horn screwed into the steering headstock and a cycle-lamp battery clipped inside the headlamp shell, to provide a rudimentary parking light.

The IG1130 flywheel carried six magnets; it could not be interchanged with the earlier Geni-mag, as this would blow out all the bulbs. Conversely, an early flywheel fitted to an IG1130 stator would not generate sufficient power. The new flywheel, Wipac number S1239, was thereafter common to all Series 55 Mk 8 generators and was marked AC/DC for easy recognition.

From August 1955 two new generators were used to replace IG1130. These were an AC lighting, spec number IG1452, identified by its having just two lighting coils and two terminal posts on the right-hand side. The other was IG1454 with an additional lighting coil and four terminal posts, although post number 2 was redundant.

With the arrival in 1956 of the swing-arm frame for the 150cc D3 Bantam Major, generator spec IG1450 replaced the IG1454 version. The only difference was the length of HT lead. IG1450 was fitted to all DC battery-lighting models up to May 1966.

Wipac did offer a conversion kit to change an AC lighting system to a full-rectified battery set. However, BSA issued a bulletin to all its service dealers in 1956 warning against fitting a conver-takit to an IG1452 unless a new IG1454 or IG1450 three-coil stator was also fitted. Machines originally wired up for an IG1130 generator but later retro-fitted with an IG1454 or IG1450 should have the yellow wire linking terminals 9 and 11 on the headlamp switch disconnected in order to limit the charge rate in the L (low) position. Confused? It gets worse.

The performance of the Series 55 Mk 8 generators gave a high-tension output of 10,000 volts at 500rpm rising to 15,500 volts at 6,000rpm. For lighting, the nominal output was rated at 30 watts. The IG1130 unit allowed a maximum day charge of 2.5 amps to pass to the battery (if fitted). On full lamp load the output was balanced out at 3,000rpm and .75 amp trickled its way out at full engine speed. The IG1450 and IG1454 generators supplied a better charge rate of 3 amps at full engine speed with a full lamp load demand matched at 2,800rpm and a trickle charge of 1.5 amps sent forth at 4,500rpm. The system worked surprisingly well, unless you were one of the unfortunates who had to push the Bantam home in the dark!

The first 175cc Bantam was the D5 Bantam Super, which appeared for the 1958 season only. Many were equipped with the basic AC IG1452 but another variant, the IG1552, soon appeared. The stator carried three lighting coils; two outer coils were connected in series and earthed at one end to provide an AC current direct to the headlamp bulb so the lights only worked if the engine was running. The larger centre lighting coil ran through a rectifier and battery to operate parking lights, stop lamp and horn. This system carried over to the revamped D7 Super Bantam of 1959 to September 1963, and then another generator came on to the scene to complement the ever-green IG1452 method. This was generator spec

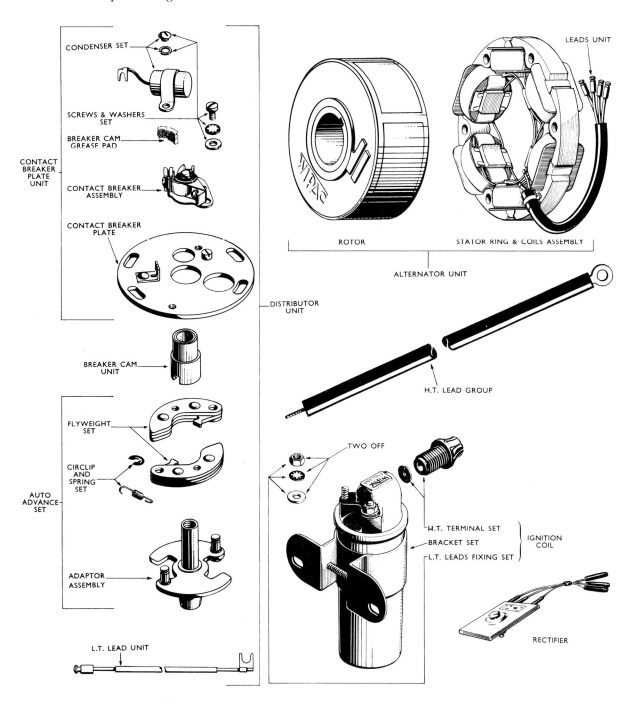

Crank-mounted alternator-type generators were introduced with the D10 model series in 1966. The points were housed on the right-hand side and the coil and rectifier were located under the seat. The extra power output was a welcome improvement, although prolonged daylight running did tend to over-charge the battery.

IG1704, similar to the IG1552 with AC lights and trickle charge, but with the ignition coil taken out of the stator plate assembly, and more conventional-looking, located under the seat. These latter Bantams could be identified by the two switches in the headlamp shell – one to control lights, the other to switch on ignition. An emergency start facility utilized the lighting coils.

Some riders encountered charging problems with the later D7 especially if constantly commuting across town with the lights on. Low engine speeds and full load resulted in an insufficient charge to the battery. In desperation, a revised cam, Wipac number S3794, with a longer points-open duration, was fitted as standard after engine number FD7 5044. The later cam should only be fitted to the two-headlamp switch D7. An alternative solution was to fit a softer 6-volt 6W/3W stop and tail bulb as opposed to the usual 6-volt 18W/3W bulb. The famous Bantam night-time 'black pause' when dipping the headlamp occurred as the switch momentarily connected both headlamp bulb filaments, and the system failed to cope with the load.

Alternator Systems and ETI

With the introduction of the D10 models, in 1966, came the change to 60-watt alternator electrical generators, which had become the standard method of supplying electrical power on motorcycles. It permitted the use of a 30/24-watt headlamp bulb, giving the sort of light intensity found on top-range 650cc twins. BSA had first used this type of system with great success in the 250cc 'C' range models as early as 1954. It was certainly a cheaper and altogether more reliable way of supplying electrical power. Alternators revitalized the performance characteristics of the Bantam. Instead of a heavy permanent magnet flywheel orbiting some coils, alternators consisted of a smaller and lighter six pole rotating magnet fixed to the crankshaft (rotor) and surrounded by six coils connected in pairs and mounted on circular laminated plates (stator). The engine was more responsive and easier to rev, with less flywheel effect. Many riders might have preferred

the calmer and less raunchy feel of the earlier models but alternators were inevitable to keep up with the demand for more powerful and efficient lighting, easier starting and more reliable parts.

A six-volt coil and rectifier occupied a space under the seat. The contactor set was now found on the right-hand end of the crankshaft, contained within a circular compartment that was sealed off from the crankcase.

For daylight running or when parking lights were switched on there was sufficient output from just one of the coil pairs. Under full headlamp lighting all three-coil pairs, connected in parallel, gave enough output to supply the bulb load and a trickle charge to the battery. The ignition switch also had an emergency start option in case the battery was flat. When the switch was set to 'E' all six coils were used to give full output to the ignition coil, provided the lighting switch was off. Once the engine had been running for a couple of minutes the ignition switch could be set to

Some of the racing ignition equipment devised especially for Bantams by Rex Caunt racing. (Courtesy Rex Caunt)

'On' and if nothing other than a low battery was the cause then lighting could be used.

Alternator systems were not without their own troubles. The usual suspects were frayed wiring, and poor or corroded connections. Electrical performance was greatly affected if through main-bearing wear the .007in air gap between rotor and stator was changed. Overheating caused the insulation of the stator coils to break down or burn out. There was no escape from the despair and frustration.

The third and final electrical system was energy transfer ignition (ETI), which even George would have been hard pressed to explain. Many Bushman models used this system and it was also found in a few D14/4 roadsters. It was a pure AC or unrectified type ignition whereby a special energy transfer coil was used in conjunction with a six-pole alternator rotor. The system was supposed to take advantage of the low-speed advantages of coil ignition and the high-speed advantages of a magneto – a sort of half-magneto, half-coil ignition. It gained something of a bad name because of its hit and miss nature and because few could understand it. Its performance depended upon accurate timing between the rotor and stator to get anything resembling a high-density spark when it was needed.

Wipac Today

With the crash of the AMC motorcycle empire in 1966 and the eventual decline of the BSA Bantam, Wipac saw the bulk of its business disappear almost overnight. Originally an American company and now with over 100 years of traumatic history behind it, Wipac concentrates solely on supplying the motor car industry with both standard factory-fitted and after-sales equipment. Since the late 1960s no manufacture of motorcycle parts has been undertaken and the factory cannot respond to questions about 50-year-old flywheel magneto generators.

George was pensioned off long ago. The model for George was an actor who would sometimes turn up at trade shows hoping to enjoy a little corporate hospitality. But that should not be allowed to spoil the myth. My Bantam packed up the other day and I remembered what George always used to say: 'Check the plug first!' True to form, it was nothing more serious than a whiskered plug and I was on my way again within a couple of minutes. As I rode away, I had the funny feeling that I was being watched by an old chap in a white coat…

7   Resurrection and Restoration

Restoring a Bantam has to be one of the easiest, most practical and rewarding projects that anyone could tackle. Bantams are not only plentiful but also have the advantage that many parts are interchangeable across the range. Any Bantam engine will fit into any Bantam frame, since they all used the same mounting lugs, even the last B175 models. Parts are plentiful and reasonably priced. (For dealers and stockists, see pages 186–188.) BSA made massive amounts of Bantams and mountains of spares, and every autojumble features piles of crankcases, cylinder heads and gearbox parts.

First Steps

The first step in rebuilding a Bantam is to locate one. The BSA Owners Club magazine *The Star*, the *VMCC Journal*, *Old Bike Mart* and *The Classic Motorcycle* are all useful sources. The choice of machinery on offer could range from a pristine ready-for-the-road example down to a cardboard box full of rusty bits and pieces. Depending upon your ability, time available, tools, resources and bank balance you have to decide what sort of project to undertake. For a first project, look for a nearly complete machine with all the mud-

Nothing can be more satisfying than a first-class restoration as shown by this 1968 D14/4 Sports finished in Flamboyant Red. (Owen Wright)

Above *This 1950 D1 Bantam De-Luxe up for sale at an autojumble would be an ideal restoration project. It is complete and original, with even the rear carrier intact. (Owen Wright)*

Left *'For sale, Bantam D3, needs slight attention otherwise good restoration project.' 866 RRE was the first bike owned by the author, and turned up at an autojumble in 1982! (Owen Wright)*

guards, fuel tank and panels in place, as the right tinware can be hard to find.

The main drawback in rebuilding a Bantam is economic. This is not something to do if you are hoping to make money. The amount you have to spend just to get a typical defunct machine through a MOT will be greater than its value. The cost of having new wheel rims re-laced, for example, is the same for a lowly Bantam as it is for a 650cc twin.

It is easy to underestimate the time and costs involved in doing a decent job and you will need to have an idea of the standard of restoration you wish to achieve. Some people like to polish the crankcases to a mirror finish. Others want a the bike that simply stays reliable. The middle way – and probably the best – involves restoring it to a good all-round 'nearly as original' condition, riding it for the next five years, taking pity on it,

cleaning it up again and then repeating the cycle. If you are on a tight budget, at least do a good job on the fuel tank, as this is the most eye-catching part of the bike. Avoid stick-on pin-striping; instead, have a go at doing your own brush-applied striping using PVC electrician's tape to mark out the lining. Some machines are now being deliberately over-restored, using a breath-taking standard of workmanship, in order to win ribbons at shows. However, the riders of the 1950s and 1960s would barely recognize these 'show bikes'. There was no polished brass or copper on the original ex-factory machines. All fittings were either painted or nickel-plated. Apart from the later 175cc De-Luxe, Supreme and

Introduced in 1965, the D7 Bantam Silver offered unbeatable value. (Courtesy Alistair Cave)

A much-modified Bantam ready for VMCC-organized trial events. (Owen Wright)

Always fit genuine spares. The reputation of the BSA Bantam was often let down by poorly produced 'pirate' parts and cheap alternatives.

Sports models, which did feature sparkling chrome and flamboyant paint finishes, the general run-of-the-mill models were hardly glamour bikes, even when brand-new.

Fittings and Finishes

The Bantam appeared with many anomalies, options and alternative fittings, and even the most diligent 'rivet counter' can be tripped up when it comes to authenticity. The tones of the D1 Mist Green paint, for example, varied enormously, as the factory bought in on a weekly basis. The original colour ranged from a leaf green that came up rich with an oily rag to a weak and watered-down eau-de-nil. The flamboyant finishes that first appeared on the mid-1960s D7 De-Luxe are very difficult to reproduce and definitely a job for the paint experts. All the tank transfers used throughout the life of the Bantam are readily

available, except the rare 'White Horse' American Trial Bronc. The toolbox carried a piled-arms transfer. Up to 1954, the text around the garter and guns read 'BSA Cycles Ltd', and thereafter it said 'BSA Motorcycles Ltd'. Such small details make all the difference.

Most restored machines are better today than when they left the factory. Some would argue, somewhat harshly perhaps, that the average engine rebuild carried out in a home garage is better than the build it would have had in Redditch, carried out by semi-skilled assemblers toiling to build 90 units per day.

Right *The way it was. A brand-new 1952 D1 gets the Kodak Box Brownie treatment. There are clues here for the restorer – no polished alloy and not much chromium plating. This bike has an unusual tubular battery container fixed to the front frame downtube. (Courtesy Mick Walker)*

Below *Restoration does not have to be totally 'as factory' authentic. This demon D1 has a Todd cylinder head, dual front brakes and electronic ignition. It is totally reliable and goes like stink! (Owen Wright)*

The engine is a delight to work with. Everything comes to pieces easily, as long as you invest in the flywheel puller and a clutch compressor. None of the parts needs any more persuasion than a gentle tap with a hide mallet. If something refuses to budge, there is a problem somewhere. When removing the cylinder barrel, remember to loosen the two screws at the crankcase mouth and when the cases are split watch out for the two hidden screws on the drive side! The gearbox and crankcase main bearings can be drifted out after the cases have been gently warmed first in hot water.

A clutch-locking tool is a useful addition, and can be made by brazing an old pair of plain and friction plates together. This tool makes it easier to undo the engine sprocket, which is located on a taper and can be stubborn. A short session with the blow torch and a proper sprocket puller is usually enough to dislodge it.

The 3/8in-pitch simplex primary chain will last for ages but it is always worth fitting a new one if the engine is stripped, and specifying a genuine Renolds replacement. Certain chains of dubious origin will soon shed their rollers and you are unlikely to spot the damage until too late. Good replacement rear chains can be found at autojumbles or bought by mail order. They are usually sold in 120-pitch lengths. Have a half-link added for a swing-arm frame model, to make fitting a lot easier.

When the cases are eventually split, make a note of any shims fitted on either side of the flywheels. Crankshaft end float should be kept

Easy restoration projects like this complete D1 can still be found, although very few will be as clean as this one. (Owen Wright)

within 0.004–0.006in. There were various arrangements of crankshaft seals. A set of new crankcase seals is an absolute must no matter how good the old ones are. Later 125cc and most 150cc engines had a fan-type impeller on the left-hand mainshaft while others had a plain collar. Make a sketch of the seal arrangement and position in the cases before removing.

The wheel hubs should also be carefully observed. It is all too easy to take the whole thing apart and then spend weeks trying to work out which spacer and washer goes where. Bantam wheels run on deep groove ball races, not the usual bicycle-type arrangement of loose balls in cups and cones. The brakes were well up to standard during their time so do not be satisfied with weak brakes; have the brake drums skimmed if they look grooved. All models should stop within about 30ft (9m) from 30mph (45km/h).

When restoring the frame, the usual damage is found on the footrest assembly. The long through bar found on D1 to D5 models is always bent and corroded. Take the opportunity to sort out the rear brake pedal bracket mounting lugs and get some new feet welded on to the centre stand!

It is frustrating to rebuild a Bantam to good presentable condition and then find it does not run well. Make sure the carburettor is good condition, fit new jets, needle and throttle slide. An in-line fuel filter is also a worthwhile addition.

Electrics

Once you have the overhauled engine and carburettor in place, you need to get the electrics right. Electricity and BSA Bantams were not the best of pals. When sorting out a Bantam the electrical system is going to be a key factor if the machine is going to be reliable. The engine build, a new paint job and new chrome plating will come to nothing if the switches and wiring are defunct. An electrical harness sometimes referred to as a loom would deteriorate after ten years even in the best of hands and a dry garage. Copper hardens with age, wires begin to fray and a green patina builds up within those PVC-covered bullet connectors. If you are rebuilding a

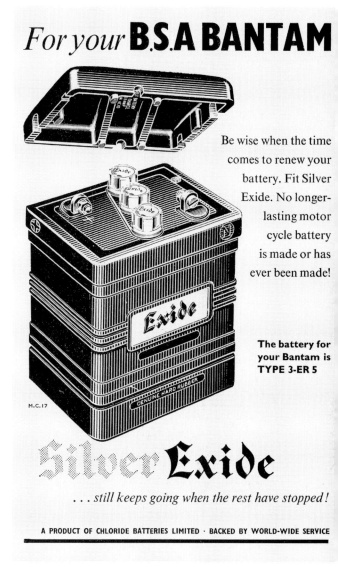

Battery-lighting Bantams were fitted with a heavy-duty Bakelite-bodied Exide battery. The cases are often used to house a modern-type battery, looking very authentic.

Bantam, re-wire it, too. Even with a new wiring harness in place make sure the earth wires are connected to a clean part of the frame.

Modern easy-to-fit electronic trigger ignition systems make tracking down old Wipac parts a pointless exercise. The first of these is the simple

Big-End Trouble

Sooner or later the inevitable would happen. To the Bantam owner it was like the day of judgement. The con-rod big-end bearing would start to make ominous metallic noises and an unbearable vibration would be felt through the handlebars and footrests. There was no accounting for when, why and how it would happen.

Replacement and repair was beyond the realm of the home mechanic. The crankshaft assembly was pressed together and required the right equipment, such as a press, a surface table, vee-blocks and a dial test indicator, as well as some valuable skill and experience. Fortunately, BSA had a nationwide network of dealers and franchised service departments, where a reconditioned spare or existing one could be turned around within a week. With the collapse of BSA and the steady decline in spares, numerous bearing reconditioning services took over. One of the most popular was that offered by Alpha Bearings in Dudley, in the West Midlands. The Alpha big-end was highly praised, came with a guarantee and was engineered better than the original. It also came with an oval-section con-rod that produced less crankcase turbulence and so offered improved performance against the original factory-fitted 'I'-section type.

Bantam owners often boasted about the longevity of their big-end bearing and a failed one was more than an irritable mishap and an inconvenient expense. It was a disaster. When the new bearing and crankshaft assembly had been re-fitted the owner would diligently swish his tank with a 16:1 petrol-oil running-in mixture and ride with sensitivity and care for at least the next 500 miles (800km). Thanks to some precision manufactured parts, the Bantam had been given a new life.

Max Nightingale of Alpha Bearings takes up the story: 'We realized during the late 1960s that there was a need for a replacement rod kit for machines other than the D1 assemblies. We produced an oval con-rod forging with the designation "Alpha 13" on the side of the stem and the original BSA reference on the other side. These rods were made of case-hardening steel and copper-plated to ensure that the heat treatment was the absolute best and a significant improvement over the original BSA rods of the period. The need for replacement rods was in answer to the inherent problem with Bantams, which wore the rod at the big-end eye on the width. The minimum width was 0.552in.

'Later we also produced a very slim polished oval-section rod, known at the factory as a "Bantam Racing rod". Unlike the Alpha 13, which was a direct replacement, the racing rod was a conversion and used a smaller crankpin raceway diameter.

'In both cases the forgings for these rods are no longer available and we have been producing a third form of replacement rod, which is an investment casting. These rods are very much more accurate than any previous

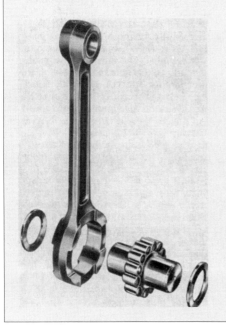

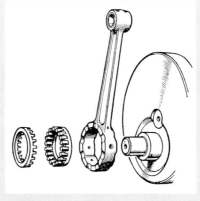

Above *The 1958 big-end bearing with duralamin roller cages and radial drillings.*

Left *The 'crowded' big-end bearing fitted with ¼in diameter × ⅜in rollers, used between 1953 and 1958.*

*Close-up of a 150cc
D3 engine. Visually, the
post-54 125cc and 150cc
unit were the same.
(Owen Wright)*

types including the BSA versions. They have been developed with racing in mind and are available for both racing and direct replacement applications. The rods are supplied with 19 and 20mm small-end eyes so that the original Torrington B910 bearing can be fitted or in racing applications a 20mm needle roller bearing.

'The cast rods are "hipped", which ensures that they benefit from the finest metallurgy, and are available from T&G Motorcycles of Milton Keynes.

'We are still able to repair any of the connecting rod types as long as they are wider than the minimum big-end width. In the repairs for all but the racing rods we re-heat treat the big-end eye and then grind it to the next oversize and fit a new crankpin with matching oversize raceway and special oversize cage and roller sets. The small end is also replaced with either the Torrington or the appropriate small end (SE24 or SE134). The Bantam racing rods have a hardened steel liner or bearing outer race fitted to the rod in place of heat-treating the rod again, and then a steel needle cage replaces the alloy cage from the original Alpha Bearings design. A new crankpin and small end are also fitted.'

Alpha Bearings also supplies replacement main shafts for all the models as these are pressed into the flywheels. The early designs from BSA have a very small timing side tip and many owners unfortunately damaged this when they remove the crank from the cases. The last 'racing' machines had shortened timing side and drive side shafts that Alpha Bearings can still supply to special order. T&G Motorcycles (*see* Useful Addresses) is still able to supply the standard shafts – probably from stock!

'Brown Atom' unit supplied by C&D Autos of Acocks Green, Birmingham (a place that is always worth a visit – a part of the city's heritage and offering plenty to Bantamites). Rex Caunt Racing offers an excellent electronic ignition set, as well as an alloy barrel and head, very popular with weekend off-road riders.

Alternatives, Options and Ancillaries

Some parts are becoming scarce. The old-type D-shaped speedometers were often robbed and used on all sorts of home-built trials and off-road bikes. Today, a number of instrument specialists will supply a reconditioned unit or carry out a first-class repair.

It is possible to fit any tank to any machine – with a little fiddling – and an early tank looks well on a D10 or D14/4. Several types were used from 1948 to 1971. D1s and D3s up to 1956 had the filler cap on the left. The D3 is the same as the D1 but the 1958 D5 is more bulbous. The jelly-mould style first appeared in 1965 and stayed until the bitter end.

Control cables usually present no problem but always check with the supplier because it is advisable to carry a spare that actually fits. Some mid- to late-1950s models used Amal twist-grips with a slightly different end fitting. A common clutch cable was fitted to D1 to D7 models; on the D10 to B175 range it was 3in (75mm) shorter. The types and lengths of front-brake cables varied according to model and year.

As for wheels, 19in rims are plentiful but D1–D3 wheels only carried thirty-six spokes instead of the normal forty. It was the same on the 18in rims fitted to D5s to B175s.

Engine and frame numbers provide the most vital clues to originality. The number of machines with replacement engines is considerable. It was once cheaper to buy a second-hand motor than to fix the old one and in these cases engine and frame serial numbers do not match. During production, random engines were placed into random frames and only the evidence of the original buff logbook and the BSA Owners Club data bank of despatch records will reveal the truth.

If you are aiming for total authenticity, the ancillaries are vital. Every machine was supplied with an inflator held under the tank and a nine-piece tool kit wrapped in a leatherette pouch went inside the toolbox. It included a 'C' spanner for undoing the exhaust nut and a small Tecalamit push-type grease gun. You won't find that on a modern Japanese bike!

One of the biggest headaches for restorers are pattern parts. A new exhaust pipe is one particular item that can cause much hardship. The golden rule in restoring is never to throw anything way. A rusty old exhaust will serve as a useful guide to check against the correct shape of a new one.

Original spark plugs for the D1 to D7 were Champion L7 or a pink-bodied Lodge HN. These are now collectors' items. Most riders fit a NGK BP6HS. The higher-compression D10 to B175 series originally called for a Champion N4, but it is possible to try a NGK B7ES; even though it is Japanese, it has been found to perform better and last much longer. Bantams were always very hard on plugs.

D1 rear parcel carriers are hard to find, as are leg-shields in restorable condition. Once a second-hand D1 or D3 passed into the hands of a teenager these and other 'old fogey' articles would be ripped from their mountings. Another prized fitting is the chrome-plated tank strips. Once a tank had been taken off for any reason, many owners did not bother to re-fit them.

When a rebuilt bike is fired up for the first time it will emit lots of smoke. Given a chance to settle down, it should eventually clear. Persistent smoking might be due to sticking piston rings or the condition of the crankcase seals; these are vital to ensure correct running. After a period of gentle running-in, undo the crankcase drain plug to release any excess oil. The fibre washer has to be in a clean condition to maintain good crankcase pressure.

Opposite *Thirty-two years after his dad bought a ratty 1956 D3 Bantam Major, Tim Wright gets presented with his own. (Owen Wright)*

Buying a Complete Bike

There is an alternative to all the angst and frustration, and all the scraping, filing, cleaning, searching, and bartering. You can simply go out and buy a complete ride-away bike. The monthly classic British motorcycle magazines usually offer a large selection, all in good running order. This is one realistic option if you want to re-live the old days and it probably works out a lot cheaper too. You might end up with a hack and struggle to get beyond the drive, but that can happen with a modern bike as well. Be wary of buying on impulse.

One thing is for certain: if you buy a Bantam, you will not be short of friends. Even if you are not the 'clubby' sort, most other owners will be eager to help, swap spares, lend tools and offer free advice.

When it comes to choosing which model the early Mist Green D1s are fast gaining the most attention and there has also been a surge of interest in ex-GPO versions. A genuine Competition D1 complete with its cylinder head decompressor is a rarity nowadays and the D10s and D14/4 Sports in original condition with flyscreen and full-width hub brakes are also worth having. The latter had a very low survival rate, since it was often mercilessly thrashed by wannabe racers.

The most sought-after model version is the Bushman. BSA made about 3,500 and most were exported. It is very easy to make a Bushman lookalike and therefore easy to buy one that is not the genuine article. There are probably more 'Bushmans' registered with the DVLC than BSA actually made.

The cheapest models appear to be D7s, mainly because of their reputation for blandness but also because so many were made. Some riders consider a Bantam an ideal second bike for getting about town. For this purpose, consider a four-speed D14/4 or the well-mannered all-rounder B175, which was especially robust.

Registration

Once your newly acquired or resurrected Bantam is ready for the road there will be some paperwork to organize especially if it needs re-registering or an age-related number. Hundreds of Bantams have lost their original registration numbers to the flourishing business of 'cherished number-plate' sales, as dealers have bought up old bikes to satisfy the vanity of their customers.

Acquiring a Registration Number
If your Bantam does not have a registration number, you will need to do the following:

• Obtain proof of the year of manufacture of the vehicle from a club or organization relevant to the make, model or type of vehicle (dating certificate). All known vehicle registrations were transferred to the DVLC in the early 1980s and old-type logbooks were replaced by a V5 document. Many old motorcycles missed the 1984 cut-off date. Newly discovered bikes can keep their original registration number provided it does not already appear on the database. If this is the case, an age-related number can be granted. The BSA Owners Club can provide a dating certificate from the original factory despatch records. Fill in and sign forms V55/5 and V765 and send two clear pictures of both sides of the bike with frame number, engine number and registration mark written on the back of each picture and signed by the claimant. Include the original logbook, old MOT certificates, tax discs or any other evidence (photocopies will only be accepted if supplied and authorized by a Vehicle Registration Office), as well as rubbings of the engine and frame numbers, to prevent fraudulent applications, and an SAE. The BSAOC usually charges a fee of about £25 for non-members. If the machine details are in order, the BSAOC will pass on the details to the DVLC for checking, processing and final approval to grant an old number.

- Arrange MOT Test Certificate and insurance cover. This can be done using the frame number.
- Contact your nearest Vehicle Registration Office (VRO) and explain what you wish to do. They may wish to inspect the vehicle.
- Complete application form V55/5 and submit to your nearest VRO together with your dating information, Test Certificate, insurance documents and appropriate licence fee.
- If the VRO is satisfied with the application they will issue an appropriate age-related registration number (non-suffix numbers are issued non-transferable). The Vehicle Excise Disc will be issued straight away. The registration document should follow within six weeks.

Passing the MOT

When it comes to putting your Bantam through an MOT there are a number of aspects to consider. Although many direct-lighting models did not have a rear brake light, all machines must now have one. Easy-to-fit pull-type switches are available and can be rigged to work from the brake rod linkage. Fitting a suitable bulb into the rear lamp is another matter. Specialists in Bantam spares will advise depending upon the type of original rear lamp fitted.

Before arranging a test, check for loose spokes, and excessive play in the forks, steering and wheels. Swing the handlebars from lock to lock and make sure the cables do not bind or the forks clout the fuel tank. The drive chain will come under scrutiny and the tester will not be impressed by a badly worn rear sprocket. Another common failure point is the angle of the brake drum lever, which often indicates the condition of the shoes. Original Dunlop Universal tyres might look authentic but you will not be allowed on the road if there are perish marks and splits in the sidewall.

The lighting supplied from a Bantam headlamp was not the most effective and you should not make the situation any worse with a dull or blistered reflector dish.

According to the current rules – but do watch out for any new legislation – the rubber bulb horn fitted to D1 and D3 direct-lighting models is legal, although some testers might take exception. Fitting a modern 6-volt AC low-power electric horn intended for mopeds is a simple enough task.

On the Road

Once your Bantam has passed its MOT, and is taxed and insured, you will have a bike that will run on the cheapest unleaded fuel at over 100mpg (2.8ltr/100km). A fully re-conditioned engine should last at least 40,000 miles (65,000km) before its next overhaul. If a long-distance tour is the object, plan on 200 miles (just over 300km) a day. You will be able to enjoy the freedom of the roads, will be able to cut through town traffic with ease and take to back lanes and dirt roads like never before. And one thing is for sure, on a Bantam you will not be frustrated by speed traps!

There is one final and very important item that will need restoring: you, the rider. If you have been out of the saddle for some years or currently ride a modern machine, the implications of piloting a Bantam should not be underestimated. Learn to ride defensively and read the situation well in advance. Do not hang too near the kerb, wear a high-visibility vest and fit a handlebar mirror. Assume every car driver cannot see you and get ready for those who pull out from junctions in front of you. Do not expect cars to give way at roundabouts and be prepared for cars that slow down and pull up alongside to get a better look. Wherever you go, heads will turn when they hear that once-familiar Bantam sound again, and as soon as you stop somebody will surely come over and say, 'A Bantam? I had one of those!'

Appendix I
BSA Bantam Production Changes

The following information is intended as a guide only. A model year usually ran from October to September. Some changes took place as early as August. Anomalies and alternative fittings abound. Fleet users such as the GPO issued their own specifications.

Year	Engine No.	Frame No.	Changes	Colours
1948	UYD-101	YD-101	Fork gaiters added after first production batches.	D1: all-over Mist Green, cream tank panels lined in red and gold. Maroon winged BSA logo. Piled-arms transfer on toolbox with 'BSA Cycles' lettering.
1949	UYD-101	YD-101	Plunger frame introduced, denoted by suffix 'S' in serial number. Centre stand held up with C-shaped link and spring instead of clip. Bantam cockerel motif introduced. Up to frame YD-2850, front wheel hub has deep counter bored to assist bearing removal. Competition D1 introduced.	D1: as 1948. Bantam cockerel transfers applied to tank panels.
1950	UYD-20001, UYDL-101 (Lucas), YD-20001, YDL-101 (Lucas)	YD1-20001 (rigid) YD1S-20001 (plunger)	De-Luxe introduced with Lucas 1A45 generator and battery lighting. From frame YD24813, exhaust pipe positioned over footrest.	As 1949.
1951	YD1-40001, YDL1-3001 (Lucas)	YD1-40001 (rigid), YD1S-40001 (plunger)	Pull and turn fuel tap replaces push-pull 'Hexagon for on' type. Amal 361/1 carburettor replaces 261/001D. De-Luxe D1 has electric horn as standard with button mounted in handlebar. Revised lighting switch, cable-operated. Up to frame YD1-57331 and YD1S-57331; fork bushes are not detachable. From engine YD1-40661 Wico-Pacy series 55 Mk 8 generator replaces Geni-mag type.	As 1950.
1952	YD1-63001 (Wico-Pacy), YD1L-8001 (Lucas)	YD1-64001 (rigid), YD1S (plunger)	Headlamp switch fitted to models with direct lighting. Steering headstock gusset strength improved.	As 1951.

Year	Engine No.	Frame No.	Changes	Colours
1953	BD2-101 (Wico-Pacy), BD2L-101 (Lucas)	BD2-101 (rigid), BD2S-101 (plunger)	Pillion footrests standard fitting. Dual seat made optional. Chrome strips added to tank ribs. Wheel rims chrome-plated. Engine numbers stamped on crankcase under carburettor instead of front mounting lug. De-Luxe D1 (Lucas) discontinued. Plunger frame; rear wheel spindle diameter increased. Tubular silencer replaces flat-Bantam type. New-style front mudguard, slim valanced and fixed to lower stanchions. Big-end bearing redesigned to incorporate 14 off ?in diam × ⅜in crowded rollers (was 12 off 7 × 7mm). Crankcase screws increased from 11 to 13.	As 1952. Black option available.
1954	D1 models: BD-101 (direct and Comp.); BDB-101 (battery). D3 models: BD3-101 (direct and Comp.); BD3B-101 (battery).	BD2-14600 (rigid), BD2S-14600 (plunger)	D1: headlamp cowl added. Tubular silencer introduced. D3 Bantam Major introduced. Large-fin engines, all models. Right-hand side crank oil seal positioned against flywheel (was located between bearings). Left-hand seal moved 0.01in outwards. Oil-way drillings allow gearbox/primary chaincase oil to lubricate RH main bearings. Thick-rim flywheels similar to previous Lucas type fitted to all models. 3 bulb stop/tail lamp fitted to battery versions. Positive earth electrics. Heavier forks for D3. Rubber damping tubes added to all forks.	D1 as 1953. Pastel Grey with cream tank panels and Bantam Major tank transfers. All wheel rims chromium-plated. 'BSA Motorcycles' type piled-arms transfer on toolbox.
1955	D1 models: DD-101 (direct and Comp.); DDB-101 (battery). D3 models: BD3-5138 (direct and Comp.); BD3B-5138 (battery).	BD2-34701 (rigid), BD2S-34701 (plunger)	Cylinder barrel and head stud centres increased to 55mm. Circlip introduced with LH crankcase seal.	As 1954. Maroon option for D1.
1956	D1 models: DD-4801 (direct); DDB-3301 (battery). D3 models: BD3-10401 (direct); BD3B-12801 (battery).	D1: BD2S-55001. D3: CD3-101.	D1 Competition and rigid frame versions discontinued. D3 has swing-arm frame only. DD and DDB engines use shims fitted to left-hand side main bearing. Crankshaft oil drag fan replaces plain collar. Fuel tank filler cap moved from LH to RH side.	As 1955.

Year	Engine No.	Frame No.	Changes	Colours
1957	D1 models: DD-4801 (direct); DDB-3301 (battery). D3 models: BD3-10401 (direct); BD3B-12801 (battery).	D1: BD2S-55001. D3: CD3-101.	Left-hand main bearing seal positioned against flywheel. Additional LH seal added. Drilings added to enable oil from gearbox to lubricate LH main bearing.	D1 as 1956. Black and Maroon options for D3.
1958	D1 models: DD-8577 (direct); DDB-7849 (battery). D5 models: ED5-101 (direct); ED5B-101 (battery).	D1: BD2S-65001. D5: FD5-101.	Model D5 Super replaces D3 Major. Crankcase studs moved out to 60mm (D5 only). New big-end bearing with Duralamin cages and radial drillings in con-rod for all models.	D1 as 1957. Maroon or black options with Bantam Super tank transfers.
1959	D1 models: DD-10812 (direct); DDB-10628 (battery). D7 models: ED7-101 (direct); ED7B-101 (battery).	D1: BD2S-67581. D7: D7-101.	Model D7 replaces D5. Completely revised frame and cycle parts. Engine has left-hand outer cover with 'Super' inscription.	D1 as 1958. D7 Super black with ivory tank panels and Bantam Super tank transfers.
1960	D1 models: DD-12501 (direct), DDB-12501 (battery). D7 models: ED7-1501 (direct), ED7B-7001 (battery).	D1: BD2S-70501. D7: D7-8101.	D1 models: frame, forks and headlamp finished in black. D7: lugs added to frame and lower steering yoke for padlock.	D1: black frame, forks, toolbox and headlamp. Tank and mudguards in Mist Green with ivory tank panels lined in red and gold. Options also in black or Fuschia Red. D7: black frame, forks, headlamp nacelle. Tank, central compartment and mudguards in Sapphire Blue, Fuschia Red or black. Ivory tank panels.
1961	D1 models: DD-14501 (direct), DDB-14501 (battery). D7 models: ED7-3001 (direct), ED7B-15501 (battery)	D1: BD2S-73701. D7: D7-18401	Red acrylic pear-shaped badges added to fuel tank. Needle roller little-end bearing replaces bronze bush.	As 1960. Fuschia Red changed to Royal Red.
1962	D1 models: DD-15481 (direct), DDB-16413 (battery). D7 models: ED7-4501 (direct), ED7B-23001 (battery).	D1: BD2S-76680. D7: D7-27450.	Con-rod small end receives needle bearing. Three extra crankcase screws added. Revised gearbox ratios and detail changes to layshaft. Rear wheel sprocket increased from 46 to 47 teeth. New silencer.	D1 as 1961.

Year	Engine No.	Frame No.	Changes	Colours
1963	D1 models: DD-16129 (direct), DDB-17606 (battery). D7 models: ED7-5505 (direct), ED7B-26904 (battery).	D1: BD2S-78746. D7: D7-33268.	D1 discontinued. Magnetic speedometers introduced. Revised silencer.	
1964	D7 models: ED7-6887 (direct), FD7-101 (battery).	D7-38400	Detail change to big-end bearing to assist lubrication. Stub form tooth profiles for gearbox.	As 1963. Chromium-plated tank panels optional extra.
1965	D7 models: ED7-9001 (direct), FD7-3001 (battery).	D7-42878	D7 De-Luxe introduced. New-style fuel tank. New-style silencer with no fish-tail. Ball-end handlebar levers. Grab handle for dual seat.	D7 De-Luxe Ruby Red with white lining on mudguards and side panels. Chromium-plated tank panels with round silver star badges.
1966	D7 models: ED7-101 (direct), FD7-9076 (battery).	D7-49855 to 51960 and CD7-101 to 8616.	D7 Super replaced by Bantam Silver. Mid-year, D10 series introduced. D10 Supreme similar to D7 De-Luxe. D10 Silver similar to D7 Silver. D10 Sports with 4-speed gearbox, racing seat, high-level exhaust and flyscreen. D10 Bushman, with 4-speed gearbox, high cradle frame, upswept exhaust, low gearing and larger rear tyre.	D7 De-Luxe as 1965. D7 Silver Blue with silver tank panels. Round silver star acrylic tank badges.
1967	D10 models: Supreme D10-101, Sports and Bushman D10A-101.	D10: Supreme D10-101, Sports D10A-101, Bushman BD10A-101.	All models fitted with Amal concentric carburettors. Heavier forks for Sports and Bushman.	All models: black frame and forks. D10 Supreme: Flamboyant Blue and chrome tank with matching blue mudguards and centre panel. D10 Silver as D7 Silver. D10 Sports as Supreme but Flamboyant Red with black and white chequered tape down centre of tank. D10 Bushman: Bushfire orange and white tank and centre panels. White mudguards.
1968	D14 models: Supreme and Sports D13B-101 to 780 and D14B-781, Bushman D13C-101 to 780 and D14C-781	D10: Supreme D13B-101 to 780 and D14B-781, Sports D13B-101S to 780 and D14B-781S, Bushman BD13C-101 to 780 and D14C-781B	D14/4 series introduced. D14/4 Supreme, D14/4S Sports and D14/4 Bushman. Large-diameter exhaust pipes. 10:1 compression ratio.	D14/4S as D10 Sports but tank base colour and chrome partitioning reversed. D14/4B as D10 Bushman.

Year	Engine No.	Frame No.	Changes	Colours

New two-letter coding introduced to denote month/year of manufacture.
A, Jan; B, Feb; C, Mar; D, Apr; E, May; G, Jun; H, Jul; J, Aug; K, Sep; N, Oct; P, Nov; X, Dec.
Year codes C, Sep 1968 to Jul 1969; D, Aug 69 to Jul 1970, E, Aug 1970 to July 1971.

Year	Engine No.	Frame No.	Changes	Colours
1969			B175 and B175 Bushman introduced Feb. Similar to D14/4. Improved crankshaft, clutch needle bearing, UNF thread forms. Central spark plug. Heavier-type forks with rubber gaiters.	B175 Flamboyant Blue as D14/4 Supreme.
1970				Flamboyant Blue, red and all-black version.
1971				Black only.

Appendix II
Badges and Transfers

Left *The famous BSA Bantam cockerel tank transfer was applied to all 125cc D1 models 1948–63.*

Left *Bantam Major tank transfer, applied to all 1954–57 150cc D3s and some early 1958 175cc D5 models.*

Right *Bantam Super tank transfer applied from 1959 to 61.*

BSA Cycles 'piled-arms' transfer applied to the toolbox and/or side panels, on all models up to 1954.

'BSA Motorcycles' 'piled-arms' transfer applied to the toolbox and/or side panels, on all models after 1954.

'Modele De-Luxe', applied to the toolbox and/or battery side panels on 175cc D7 De-Luxe Bantams.

Bantam D14/4, applied to the side panels on the 175cc D14/4 Supreme.

Bantam D14/4S, applied to the side panels on the 175cc D14/4S Sports.

Piled-arms transfer, applied to rear number-plate bracket on all models.

Bantam 175, applied to the side panels on 1969–71 B175 models.

Bushman tank panel motif, applied to all Bushman models from 1966

Left *The circular acrylic silver star tank badges first appeared on the 1965 D7 Super De-Luxe and were used on all models up to 1971. (Owen Wright)*

Below *The red pear-shaped acrylic tank badges were first used on BSA models with the introduction of the 1958 250cc C15, and became the standard motif for most other models. They were applied to the 1961 Bantam D7 range but were eventually replaced by the silver stars in 1965. (Owen Wright)*

Bibliography

Bacon, Roy, *BSA Gold Star and Other Singles* (Osprey Collector's Series, 1982, ISBN 0 85045 447 6)

Information on the Bantam within the chapter on 'Other Singles', following the production history format with technical information appendices. Not easy to follow but worth adding to any collection.

Bacon, Roy, *BSA Singles Restoration* (Niton Publishing, 1988, ISBN 1 85579 023 8)

Out of print but worth tracking down. Full of detail for people who want to restore to a good standard.

Bacon, Roy, *BSA Bantam All Models 1948–1971* (Niton Publishing, ISBN 1 85648 311 8)

Now out of print. Part of the 'monograph' series, a good small book on the history of Bantams.

Bell, A. Graham, *Two-Stroke Performance Tuning* (Haynes Publishing, ISBN 1 85960 619 9/213)

Clew, J.R., *BSA Bantam Workshop Manual* (J.H. Haynes & Co, 1973, SBN 0 85696 006 3)

Another Bantamite's must-have that has served thousands of home mechanics. The first Haynes motorcycle title published and still in print. The format is the usual Haynes 'picture gallery' of step-by-step strip-down and re-assembly. The machine depicted is a D7 Super but there is ample help for D1, D3, D5 and the later four-speed machines. Also covers all the various electrical systems used, from Geni-mag to alternator.

Clew, Jeff, *BSA Bantam Super Profile* (Haynes, 1983, ISBN 0 85429 333 7)

Out of print but sometimes turns up at auto-jumbles. Contains a production history and some very interesting photographs.

Haycraft, H.C., *Book of the BSA Bantam* (Pitman, last edition 1966)

Out of print but easily found at autojumbles. Excellent pocket-sized book for anyone buying a second-hand Bantam, packed with detail – information, photos and drawings, and technical data. Has stood the test of time.

Robinson, John, *Motorcycle Tuning – Two Stroke* (Butterworth Heinemann, ISBN 0 75061 80 X/228)

Wilson, Steve, *Practical British Lightweight Two-Stroke MotorCycles* (Haynes, 1990, ISBN 0 85429 709 X)

An all-time favourite, containing a well-written and lengthy chapter about the Bantam. Witty and informative, and written by a true Bantamite who rode a D7 to Crete and back.

Original BSA service manual sheets for the Bantam are often found at autojumbles, and are also readily available from the listed booksellers.

Bantam Websites

www.mistgreen.com
Australian site well worth a visit, full of news, pictures and information.

www.communigate.co.uk
The home of the BSA Bantam Virtual Club: 'No clubhouse, no subscription, no committee, no hassle.' Try it out!

www.horgis.co.uk
David Horgan displays his own restoration project.

www.freeweb.pdq.net/kapuni/bsa/bsa.html
Definitely up-beat, with Bantams anywhere and everywhere.

www.netcomuk.co.uk/~carol-h/index.html
Details of an ex-GPO D1 restoration project, with plenty of useful information.

Useful Addresses

Clubs for Bantam Owners

(Details correct at time of publication.)

BSA Owners Club (BSAOC)
PO Box 27
Crewe
Cheshire CW1 6GE
Membership Secretary: Brian Connelly
E-mail: bsaocmembsec@waitrose.com
Website: www.bsaoc.demon.co.uk

The BSAOC is an international organisation with associated clubs all over the world. In the UK over twenty branches meet on a regular basis and membership is open to anyone who owns a BSA motorcycle. 'Bantamites' form an integral part of the club's activities.

The BSAOC was founded by a group of enthusiasts in Sheffield in 1958. Others soon followed, in Nottingham, Birmingham and Surrey. By 1960 there were eight or nine individual

The annual BSA Owners Club National Field Day rally always attracts plenty of Bantams! (Owen Wright)

groups, all operating different sets of rules, sub-scription rates and 'aims and objects'. Eventually a national club was formed and began producing *The Star*, a monthly magazine crammed with news, views, stories and for sale/wanted adverts. The club's many services include a transfer scheme, an extensive library of books, technical literature and photos, as well as a wide range of technical consultants.

The club has always had an active programme of outdoor events with the highlight being the international rally, held in a different country every year, providing the opportunity for mem-bers of European clubs to meet for a week's hol-iday. Other important events in the calendar are the TT meet, the annual field day and the dinner dance, at which club awards are presented.

The club is made up of enthusiasts from all over the world who have got together for their mutual benefit, at international, national and local level, to compete with riders of similar machines on equal terms, and to discuss matters of com-mon interest. Most important of all, since the clo-sure of the BSA factory, the club aims to preserve the motorcycles that bear the BSA name.

The British Two-Stroke Club
259 Harlestone Road
Duston
Northampton NN5 6DD
Membership Secretary: Mrs Lynda Tanner
Website: www.btsc.btinternet.co.uk

The British Two-Stroke Club was started in 1929 by a group of enthusiasts, with the intention of encouraging the use of two-stroke powered motorcycles, mainly small-capacity models. In

motorsports, two-stroke machines had been at a disadvantage by being grouped together with much larger four-stroke machines. A prominent founder member of the club was T.G. (Tommy) Meeten, a former TT rider and competitor in the Scottish and International Six Days Trials. Impressed by the performance of a diminutive Francis-Barnett model, which he had ridden in a trial (without any great expectations), he decid-ed to campaign two-stroke machines in prefer-ence to the much larger four-strokes that may well have brought him more recognition.

The BTSC enjoyed a revival in the early 1980s thanks to an increasing interest in old motorcy-cles. From then on the club has mainly been biased towards people who are interested in keeping and running old two-stroke motorcycles on the road. The club still has a very strong Vil-liers following, but it encompasses all makes of two-stroke machines (not just those of British manufacture), and also those of all ages. The BSA Bantam is well supported in the BTSC, with its own expert consultant.

The Vintage Motor Cycle Club
Allen House
Wetmore Road
Burton Upon Trent
Staffordshire DE14 1TR
UK
Telephone: +44 1283 540557
Fax: +44 1283 510547
Website: www.vmcc.net

On 28 April 1946, a band of 38 enthusiasts assembled at the Lounge Cafe, Hog's Back, Guildford, Surrey, with the object of forming a motorcycle club for owners of machines manufactured prior to December 1930. 'Titch' Allen, the instigator of the meeting, took the chair and outlined his ideas. His main object was to promote the use and preservation of vintage machines and from his vision the Vintage Motor Cycle Club was formed.

Those founder club members have made an enormous contribution to the preservation of motorcycling history. Membership today stands at nearly 14,000, but there has been no loss of the camaraderie or helpfulness usually associated with smaller clubs.

Post Office Vehicle Club
Contact: Chris Hogan
The Brownings
3 Tallowood
Lower Charlton
Shepton Mallet
Somerset BA4 5QN
Website: www.poveclub.org.uk
Secretary: John Taggart, 7 Bignall Rand Drive, Wells, Somerset BA5 2EV

A unique society dedicated to preserving General Post Office vehicles.

Bantam Racing Club
If you really want to learn how to make a Bantam fly, why not take up Formula Bantam racing?

Race Entries Secretary:
J. Allison
25 Herthull Road
Thurnby Lodge
Leicester LE5 2EL
Website: bsabantamracing.tripod.com/index.html

The BSA Bantam Club
In order to satisfy the upsurge of interest in the Bantam a dedicated club was formed in May 2002. Already a lively monthly magazine, *Bantam Banter*, has been launched.

Details from: Ann Hook
Flat 2, 4 St Nicholas Place
Sheringham
Norfolk NR26 8LE

Alternatively, contact Lynne Marshall, e-mail: MMarshall23@compuserve.com

Bantam Spares

General Spares

Bantam John
18 Bowshaw
Dronfield
Sheffield S18 6GB
Tel/Fax: 01246 290021

'Bantam John' Phelan has extensive stocks of spares and an in-depth knowledge of BSA Bantams. Look out for the familiar yellow jerseys at autojumbles!

Bri-Tie (Mail Order)
Cwmsannan House
Llanfynydd
Carmaarthen
Dyfed SA32 7TQ
Tel/Fax: +44 1558 668579
E-mail: Enquiries@britiemotorcycles.com

Polly Palmer, a long-time devotee of all things BSA, and Vice President of the BSAOC, is a regular at autojumbles and provides a speedy and efficient spares mail order service. His speciality is supplying tins of paint in all the colours ever found on a Bantam.

C&D Autos
1193/9 Warwick Road
Acocks Green
Birmingham B27 6RG
Tel: 0121 706 2902

The Croft boys' shop is well worth a visit and provides a superb mail order supply. They can provide the Brown Atom electroinc ignition module already sold to hundreds of Bantam owners.

Draganfly Motorcycles
The Old Town Maltings
Broad Street
Bungay
Suffolk NR35 1EE
Telephone: +44 1986 894798/892826 (2 lines)
Fax: +44 1986 894798
E-mail: spares@draganfly.co.uk
Website: www.draganfly.co.uk

Draganfly was once the main suppliers of Ariel spares but has since bought up tons of BSA parts.

A. Gagg & Sons
106 Alfreton Road
Nottingham NG7 3NS
Tel/Fax: 0115 978 6288
E-mail: gagg@mail.com
Website: www.gagg-and-sons.freeserve.co.uk

A long-established business with plenty to offer Bantam owners.

Kidderminster Motorcycles
60–62 Blackwell Street
Kidderminster
Worcs DY10 2EE
Telephone: 01562 66679
Fax: 01562 825826

Another popular autojumble regular offering a mail order spares service.

Malcolm Leech (mail order)
Tel: 0121 559 7306 (Warley, West Midlands)

Specializing in Bantams, especially those 'hard to find' parts. Excellent for electrical spares, new and used parts. Although Malcolm provides a mail order service he often attends classic motorcycle autojumbles throughout the UK.

Merlin Spares
E-mail: info@merlinspares.co.uk

Makers of reproduction 'flat Bantam' silencers.

T & G Motorcycles (mail order)
1 Slated Row
Old Wolverton Road
Old Wolverton
Milton Keynes
Bucks MK12 5NJ
Telephone: 01908 698 484

Still one of the first names in Bantam spares, offering many new and used parts; exchange cranks, etc.

Ian Laycock Motors
Telephone: 01724 847111 (Scunthorpe, Lincs)

Many new and used parts.

Len Baker (Old British Bike Shop)
Telephone: 01502 724488 (Suffolk)

D1/3 nut and bolt kits, engine spares, paint etc.

Speedometers

Dave Booth
Telephone: 01243 378447

Reconditioned 'D' chronometric speedometers.

A.E. Pople
52 Henley Drive
Frimley Green
Surrey GU16 6NF
Tel/Fax: 01252 835353
E-mail: a.pople@ntlworld.com
Website: www.speedorepairs.co.uk

David Woods
La Casita
Church Lane
Eastergate
Chichester
West Sussex PO20 6UZ
Telephone: 01243 542521
E-mail: Davidwoods@chronometrics.fsnet.co.uk
Website: www.chronometricspeedos.co.uk

Chronometric speedometer repair service and part exchange service.

Seats

R.K. Leighton
Unit 3, Gunsmith House
50–54 Price Street
Birmingham B4 6JZ
Telephone: 0121 359 0514
Fax: 0121 333 3130
E-mail: infor@rk-leighton.fsnet.co.uk
Website: www.rk-leighton.co.uk

High-quality re-upholstery service and 'fit-it-yourself' seat cover kits.

Racing

Rex Caunt Racing
Unit 6, Kings Court
Kingsfield Road
Barwell
Leics LE9 8NZ
Telephone: 01455 846963
Fax: 01455 846963
Website: www.rexcauntracing.com

Electronic ignition, alloy barrel and cylinder head kits. The ultimate for trials Bantams.

Petrol Tank Repairs

John Yeats
Tel/Fax: 01865 361644 (Oxford)

Petrol tanks restored, painted and lined to owners' specifications.

Wheels and Tyres

Central Wheel Components
8 & 9 Station Road
Coleshill
Birmingham B46 1HT
Telephone: 01675 462264
Fax: 01675 466412
E-mail: infor@central-wheel.co.uk
Website: www.central-wheel.co.uk

Wheel lacing, spoke sets, tyres, rims, etc.

Hagon
7 Roebuck Road
Hainault
Essex IG6 3JH
Telephone: 020 8502 6222
Fax: 020 8502 6274
E-mail: slaes@hagon-shocks.co.uk
Website: www.hagon-shocks.co.uk

Lambrook Tyres
PO Box 44
Honiton
Devon EX14 4YP
Tel/Fax: 01404 891 189
E-mail: sales@lambrooktyres.com
Website: www.classictyres.com

Index